Praise for Gabrielle Glancy's
The Art of the College Essay

Gabrielle Glancy has written an innovative, entertaining, utterly brilliant how-to guide on writing college essays that will revolutionize the art of teaching writing. I read the book in one night and laughed all the way through. She's funny. And super insightful! For students, counselors, parents, writers of all kinds and just plain everyday people who want to know how to write from the inside out, this book is the light at the end of the tunnel.

—Yael Kropsky, Former Development Coordinator at Scholastic Books Entertainment, Digital Content Expert

Readable, funny and smart, *The Art of the College Essay* takes the anxiety out of the writing process and replaces it with a completely organic, common sense way of getting to the heart of what you're trying to say. It is **the** book on the subject of writing college essays.

—Jessica Brenner, Columbia University, Independent College Counselor

Why didn't someone tell me what Gabrielle Glancy seems to know by instinct when I was writing my college essay? Not only does she give practical advice, but in the lightest, most playful way possible, Glancy has an almost spiritual take on the process. It's a real twenty-first century guide to the whole college essay phenomenon.

—Melissa Feuerstein, Research Associate, Davis Center, Harvard University

The Art of the College Essay is groundbreaking. No one has even come close to articulating what Gabrielle Glancy proposes in this book—that you must get lost in order to get found. Glancy teaches students how to get it all out in the worry-free zone of The Free Write, and then go back to read what they've written to see what they're trying to say. Most guides tell you to do it the other way around. That's a recipe, as Glancy puts it, for *that which shall not be named—writer's block. The Art of the College Essay* will change the landscape of college essay writing—and the teaching of writing in general. This book is a gift to the world.

—Illana Berger, PhD, Living the Sacred

Finally, some insight into writing the college essay that offers no pretense. A wonderful read—alive, funny and refreshingly real—*The Art of the College Essay* shows writers what it means to find wisdom in experience and to persuade real readers by being utterly humane. Glancy gets into and under the art of writing the college essay like no one I've ever seen.

—Erick P. Gordon, PhD, Former Director of the New York City Writing Project, Founder of Student Press Initiative, Teachers College, Professor, Columbia University

The Art of the College Essay had me at the first sentence. Glancy's writing is powerfully direct, a hand reaching out to grab you by the collar. You can do this, she tells us. I'll show you how. She knows her stuff backwards and forwards: how to do battle with the blank page, how to overcome our own worst impulses, and most of all, how to write an essay "so gripping, so authentic, and so real, that the admissions director cannot, much as she may want to, turn away."

—Erin Van Rheenen, Senior Writer and Editor at the San Francisco Exploratorium, Author of *Living Abroad in Costa Rica*, Former High School English Teacher, University High School, San Francisco

I learned the art of teaching writing from Gabrielle Glancy. Her insights into the creative process—and how to tap into the deep reserves in all of us—are remarkable. *The Art of the College Essay* will serve as an indispensable guide not only for students writing their college essays, but for anyone who wants to learn to write.

–Clifford Chase, Author of *Winkie* and *The Tooth Fairy*, Director, Creative Writing Program, Wesleyan University

Gabrielle Glancy has developed a unique and organic method of empowering students to dig deep within themselves to find their own inner voice. Using the methods outlined in *The Art of the College Essay*, my son blossomed as a creative thinker who trusts his instincts, ideas and impressions of our shared human experience. As a parent and academic engaged with student writing, I fully endorse the way *The Art of the College Essay* demystifies the writing process. This book is a gem.

–Paula Birnbaum, Ph.D., Academic Director of Art History & Museum Studies, University of San Francisco.

Filled with real-life examples and tried-and-true exercises, this book offers insight and encouragement every step of the way, without ever feeling prescriptive. Whether the prospect of writing about yourself fills you with dread or delight, *The Art of the College Essay* will serve as a wise and worthy companion throughout the journey.

–Nancy Boutilier, Visiting Assistant Professor of Rhetoric & Composition, Oberlin College

Gabrielle Glancy's students will never, never forget her. Her gift is not simply the dedication of the inspired teacher; it is the uncompromising truth of genius, the laser-like insight of honesty and the courage of the divine.

–Stanley Bosworth (1927-2011), Visionary, Founder & Former Head of The Saint Ann's School for Gifted and Talented, New York City

The Art of the College Essay

SECOND EDITION

Gabrielle Glancy

ONEIRIC
PRESS

Oneiric Press
www.newvisionlearning.org

Book Layout ©2016 Tracy R. Atkins
Book Cover by Damonza
The Free Write™ trademark Oneiric Press

The Art of the College Essay / Gabrielle Glancy.—2nd ed.
Paperback: 978-0-9973529-1-7
Kindle/ebook: 978-0-9973529-2-4

Contents

Preface to the Second Edition 1

From the Other Side of the Table 5

The How, What, Where and Why of It 13

   Who Is This Book Written For? 16

   How Is This Book Organized? 19

   A Note on Product and Process 19

   How Do You Use This Book Most Effectively? 21

Product 23

   1. Oh, the Places You Can Go! 23

   2. Why Not Just Say It Directly? 34

   3. What Exactly Is a Narrative Personal Statement, Anyway? 36

   4. Why Do Colleges Want Narrative Essays? 38

   5. What Is a Story? 39

   6. What Do You Mean by Reflection? 40

   7. What Makes a Great Story Great? 42

Process 47

   1. What to Write About—That Is the Question— or Is It? 47

   2. If I Don't Begin with a Topic, How Do I Begin? 53

   Plan A: A List of Significant Moments 54

   Plan B: Play the Five-Adjective Game: 57

   Plan C: The Interview 61

   3: Preparing the Soil 65

   Plan D: Wishes, Lies and Dreams 72

   4: The Free Write™ 80

   The Four Modes of Writing: 88

   5. The Expanded Free Write 91

   6. How to Make Order Out of Chaos 95

   7. Techno-Logy 103

   8: RE-Vision 111

9. What Kind of Language Makes Strong Writing Strong?............ 116

10. Proofreading 120

The Slight Edge 123

What's a Parent to Do? 127

Afterword: The Art of Writing the College Essay 131

Appendix A: Sample Prompts.. 133

Common App 135

Tufts... 135

The University of California 137

Stanford... 141

Hampshire College 141

M.I.T. 142

Occidental College... 143

Princeton University 143

Appendix B: Adjectives That Describe Personal Qualities 145

Appendix C: Quick Guide to Writing a Winning College Essay
.... 151

Appendix D: Dos and Don'ts in the World of Grammar 155

Appendix E: Model Essays 159

Cat in the Hat Hat 159

Las Tres Sofias 160

Egyptian Rat Slap & Blueteeth 162

Dendrochronology.. 164

Finding My Sea Legs... 166

Grandpa Stephen 168

Heller Keller: A Place of Power 170

Mighty Minnows.. 171

Mudville 173

There Are Cows in the Story... 175

Traveling is a Part of Me... 176

One Road, Many Roads 178

Appendix F: Trouble-Shooting Guide...................................... 181
About Gabrielle Glancy... 183

Some of the content in this book was originally developed on my website: www.newvisionlearning.org. If you visit the website, you can participate in the ongoing conversation there about the college process, the challenges of and tricks to succeeding in school and getting into college, and the world of college admissions in general. To find out more about my services, please feel free to contact me at gabglance@gmail.com.

Disclaimer: The information contained in this book represents the views of the author at time of publication. It is recommended that the reader determine whether this information is applicable to his or her own situation and to what, if any, use the information in this book should be put. Though some of the scenes resemble actual experiences, they are fictionalized and names have been changed except when a student has given permission to use his or her essay or excerpted pieces thereof.

Acknowledgments

Over and over my students have amazed me with their courage and dedication. They have trusted me with their stories and with their journey to find them and articulate them in the form of the college essay. For this, I am honored and grateful.

For his belief in this project, deep friendship, and meticulous reading of the book, thanks to Clifford Chase.

I am also grateful to Joel Friedlander, Damonza Book Design, Tracy Atkins, Eva Tuschman, Kevin Bentley, Laura Jacoby, Meg Allen, David Richo, Cesar Aira, Jeff Olson, my son, Marco, who daily teaches me "the art of patience," and Tanya Baker and The National Writing Project—and to everyone who has helped this book become a reality.

And thanks to Margaret Crastnopol, ever my muse.

The creative is the place where no one else has ever been. You have to leave the city of your comfort and go into the wilderness of your intuition. What you'll discover will be wonderful. What you'll discover is yourself.

—*Alan Alda*

Preface to the Second Edition

One day, soon after the first edition of *The Art of the College Essay* came out, I was practicing the lost art of browsing in a bookstore, when I came upon the title, *The Slight Edge: Turning Simple Disciplines into Massive Success & Happiness*, by a man named Jeff Olson.

Before even cracking open the book, I had a strong sense I would know what was inside. Perhaps I had not organized my thoughts on the subject the way Olson has done in his book, nor had I even articulated to myself, nor to my students, exactly what it takes to achieve a *slight edge*, but I knew that I would recognize the basic principles involved, because I had been helping students find the slight edge in pursuit of their dreams for almost thirty years—and I had seen, in my own life, how the smallest things have made the biggest difference.

Turning straw into gold is alchemy, just as writing a college essay that opens the door to your future turns a blank page into a winning lottery ticket. And there is a *qualitative*, not quantitative, difference between going through the motions, waving your wand, and knowing what to do.

If the process were simply mechanical, such as you might find in a guide to assembling Ikea furniture—"Place x and y in front of z, slide and turn"—I would be out of a job, and life would be out of one of its great mysteries.

Success, in getting into college and in life, involves as much inspiration as it does perspiration, and sometimes a little more perspiration than you might have thought necessary. I was lucky to learn this very early, perhaps in the fourth grade, when I saw that doing just a tiny, tiny little bit more than everyone else, resulted in my reaping rewards far greater.

1

For this reason, I have decided to include a chapter in this book addressing the slight edge in college essay writing and admissions. While it was implicit in the earlier edition of this book, I thought it would be useful to make it explicit now. You will find this chapter towards the end of the book, following the chapter on Proofreading.

I have also watched myself, even more closely than before I published the first edition of this book, to see what it is I actually do—by instinct, and through years of experience—that helps students be so successful.

What I saw is that I follow my own advice—generally—but that when a moment calls for a different approach, perhaps a yet-untried strategy or idea—I go with it.

I remember years ago when I was a fledgling teacher—I was in my early twenties—leading a class in a frog dissection or teaching my students how to conjugate the verb *etre* (I was teaching Biology, French and English at the time.) I could see against the slate gray building that flanked the back windows of my classroom, the first snowflakes of the year, falling tenderly, I would say almost questioningly, from the sky.

The students must have seen my amazement, for they turned around, almost in unison, to catch a glimpse of what had obviously entranced me.

At moments such as these, back in the day when I was a student, the teacher would demand that we "turn around and pay attention!"

But actually, that's exactly what my students and I were doing.

It was snowing, the first snow of the year, and it was beautiful. We *were* paying attention—to the moment at hand.

In writing, and in teaching writing, one must be open to see, and willing to go, where the river takes you. Sometimes this means trying a different strategy, one that may seem to come out of left field. I have included some suggestions for these in the chapter entitled *Wishes, Lies and Dreams.*

You will find this chapter particularly helpful if you are stuck before you even get started, and cannot think of what to write about. This chapter offers some out-of-the-box suggestions, which will help loosen the soil, and may lead to the sprouting of some heretofore unimagined seeds of thought.

I have also included a new section in which I delineate, even more clearly, what I call *The Four Modes of Writing: Showing, Telling, Analyzing and Reflecting*—and go into much more detail about what the all-hallowed *Showing* actually involves.

I also offer a bit more advice about what to do when you're faced with word limits. In this section, I advise that you "Roll out the dough before you cut the cookies." You can find a more detailed explanation in the section with this title.

You will also find a new chapter on the uses of technology (Skype, IM, Google Docs, Screen Sharing) in the teaching of writing.

And finally, I speak to the deeper aspects of success—in writing, in paving the way to a successful journey applying to college, and in achieving success and finding happiness in whatever you endeavor. You will find these reflections in the chapter, *The Slight Edge*.

In addition, I have included some new and excellent samples of winning essays, to use as models, and for inspiration. You will find these sprinkled throughout the book and/or in Appendix E.

It is my hope that reading this book will, at the very least, give you a slight edge—or even more than a slight edge—and will help you find your own unique path to success.

From the Other Side of the Table

It was like crossing over, behind the curtain of darkness, through the mystery world that lies between this life and the next, when I was given the rare opportunity to work in college admissions and read student essays from the other side of the table.

I had already been in the business of helping students realize their dreams for almost twenty years by that point. I had probably helped hundreds, if not thousands, of students, here and abroad, navigate the college process and think about and fashion winning college essays.

But reading them for real, where it counts—and being tasked with the awesome responsibility of choosing which students get in and which do not—was downright eye-opening.

What I saw was that among the multitude of essays that passed across my desk, there were only a precious few that I read from beginning to end—and these almost in spite of myself.

If you could be a fly on the wall of an admissions director, here is what you would see:

He or she sits down with a pile of folders. In them are contained the recommendations, grades, SAT scores, and essays of hundreds of prospective students. Here they are, all those shining stars, those amazing three-dimensional beings, eager to please, in little more than black and white on the page (or screen, as the case may be).

It's going to be a long day plowing through these applications!

What's an admissions director to do?

She stretches, sighs, stretches again, and prepares for the monumental task ahead.

OK, here we go. The elaborate ceremony involved in *preparing to be bored*!

And bored she will be.

Yawn. Yawn. Time for another sip of coffee? Another stretch? Oh, that's interesting. Who's that walking by outside the window?

And then it happens. The unimaginable. As if by some miracle, the first sentence of a student's essay leaps off the page, wrestles the cup of coffee out of her hands, and grabs her by the collar.

For a moment there is a struggle. Boredom, once again, almost wins.

But something else takes over.

There is something so powerful in the way the essay is written—so gripping, so authentic, so real—that the admissions director cannot, much as she may want to, turn away.

Against all odds, she *actually* reads every single word of the essay.

When she is finished, she pauses for a second. Visibly moved, she turns to her associate, say, who is cleaning the dirt from under his fingernails.

She looks at him.

He looks back at her.

He knows what is happening. He knows the unimaginable has happened because, once in a blue moon, it has happened to him.

"No?" he says.

"Yes," she says.

She passes him the essay. The same powerful arm that came off the page and gripped her by the collar, has grabbed ahold of him, too.

Will this student be accepted to the University of X, Y or Z?

Let's put it this way. His chances are a heck of a lot better than those of a student who has provided the admissions committee (Ad Com) with what it expected to find—boredom.

Recently, a colleague of mine who for many years was director of college counseling at a prestigious high school and, before that, worked in admissions at Washington University, St. Louis, had this to say after reading tens of thousands of college essays:

> I was overwhelmed by the number of bland, formulaic, and trite essays; I know admissions people have been complaining for some time about the deteriorating quality of essays: the unwillingness of kids to take chances—and unfortunately, this is what I found too. I was struck by the number of essays that seemed to be straight out of an English class assignment folder; the number that tried to be cutesy (mistaking cute for creative); the number that were either travelogues and didactic, showing no glimpse of the person behind the writing; the number that were exercises in self-praise; and the number of those that were "hardship" documents that showed little or no effort to communicate how all this hardship had been processed.

Sigh...I wish I could say it weren't true.

But the fact is, very few students know how to write an essay that will do what it needs to: tip the scales in their favor.

Does the essay matter that much?

The Essay Matters

I was preparing to tell the story about my experience of working in admissions at a conference at which I was invited to speak on, you guessed it, "The Art of the College Essay," when this guy wearing a rumpled suit and a University of Chicago baseball cap comes in and noses around my pamphlet table.

He was kind of hemming and hawing, making sounds, picking things up and putting them down. He stood a long time looking over my materials. I watched him pick up my card, turn over my brochure, fiddle with my pens. Under his University of Chicago hat, I saw he had no hair. I also noticed he didn't have eyebrows.

Finally, he turned to me. "Can I have one of your pens?" he said.

"Of course," I said.

"Thanks," he said and started walking towards the door.

When he was just about out of the room, he turned back towards me, "So what's your talk about anyway?"

"The Art of the College Essay," I answered.

"Ohhh, I see," he said. Suddenly, his eyebrow-less eyes lit up.

"I've got a story to tell you," he said. He let the door go and came back into the room. "The other day I was waiting for a table at this bar in a restaurant. I struck up a conversation with the guy next to me. He was waiting for a table, too. Seemed like a nice guy. He said, 'What do you do?' I told him I was a dermatologist. He told me he was admissions director at the University of Chicago. 'My daughter goes there,' I said. He asked me her name. I told him. He told me *he* was the guy who got my daughter *into* the University of Chicago. What are the chances of that?"

"No kidding!" I said.

"Yeah," he said. "Ya know what else? He told me it was her *essay* that got her in."

"Oh my God," I said. "Can you stick around and tell the group of people I'm about to address the story you just told me?"

It was like this guy had popped out of my imagination—I kinda had to pinch myself—and was reflecting back to me what I already knew and what I was just about to say in my talk.

The eyebrow-less man suddenly got shy. "No," he said. "I've got to run. I've got a plane to catch." In a rumpled suit and wearing that University of Chicago baseball cap, he didn't look like he was about to catch a plane. But what could I do?

This time when he opened the door, he actually let himself out.

A few minutes later, I told his story to the room of people who had come to hear me speak. They looked a little incredulous. It was improbable, but it had just really happened.

What the eyebrow-less man said was true.

The essay does matter.

In fact, it's one of the most important pieces of the college admissions puzzle.

Without it, you would be just numbers (your GPA and ACT/SAT scores) on a page with a list of extracurricular activities.

Not to depress you, but there are thousands of 4.4 students out there with near-perfect scores on their SATs vying for a chance to go to University X, Y, or Z.

Actually, this is encouraging news. Why? Because not all of them get in.

It's not all about grades and test scores.

It's also encouraging because you can do something about it.

> **The essay piece of the admissions puzzle
> is something you can control.**

By the time you write that essay, your grades and test scores are a *fait accompli*. They've already happened. You did what you could. You did your best—although I would strongly suggest you keep your grades up and retake the SATs after getting some good help, if you think you can significantly improve your scores.

In fact, the essay is the *only* place you have total control. It's crucial you take advantage of this opportunity. You have to realize that what I just told you is not a secret. The Ad Com knows it, too! What this means is that everyone knows you have as much time as you need to write the best essay(s) you can.

If your essays are half-baked and full of errors—it's your way of saying, "I don't really care that much."

Because, theoretically, you could have written countless more drafts before pressing "send."

Recently, I came upon an article in Boston.com on the subject.

I was baffled by this article because it starts out by saying that a student's GPA and test scores are the most important pieces of the college application, yet it ends by saying that, on the other hand, the essay, which is the only piece the student can control, is more important than you'd think:

> While the essays are important, they say, it is the transcript that is the most important factor in deciding whether to admit a student.
>
> The rigor of courses selected, how a student did in those courses, and standardized test scores are the first considerations.
>
> Then, all things being equal, an essay can tilt the balance in either direction, especially at the more selective schools.
>
> "The essay lets us know, who is this person behind the numbers? Will they contribute?" Mahoney said.

At selective schools, applicants are often very similar in academic achievements and extracurricular activities. In these cases, essays take on added importance.

http://www.boston.com/mt/yourcampus/college-bound-boston/2013/10/from_the_pros_best_college_ess.html

How do you tilt the balance in your favor? You write an essay from the heart, in your own voice, that tells *your* story and that stops the Ad Com in its tracks. You job is to come alive in front of the people reading your essays—like teleporting crew members in *Star Trek*, your glittering beams of light must take shape before them.

Your essay must take two dimensions and turn them into three. Even four.

That's alchemy, you might say. Magic.

It kinda is.

> You see I'm trying in all my stories to get the feeling of the actual life across—not to just depict life—or criticize it—but to actually make it alive. So that when you have read something by me you actually experience the thing. You can't do this without putting in the bad and the ugly as well as what is beautiful. Because if it is all beautiful you can't believe it. Things aren't that way. It is only by showing both sides—3 dimensions and if possible 4 that you can write the way I want to.
>
> —Ernest Hemingway, On Writing

There seems to be some consensus about the goal of good writing. Here's what the great Southern novelist William Faulkner had to say on the subject:

> The aim of every artist is to arrest motion, which is life, by artificial means and hold it fixed so that a hundred years later, when a stranger looks at it, it moves again...
>
> —William Faulkner

OK, I get it. The essay matters, and my writing must bring my experience to life. But *how* do you write one of the essays this article describes? That's what this book is about.

PART I

The How, What, Where and Why of It

What is this book about? Who is it for? Why should I believe you? How is this book organized?

Sometimes I feel more like a shaman than a college counselor. To write an amazing essay, one that will knock the socks off whoever reads it—and that's what it takes to tip the scales in your favor—you have to take an amazing journey.

As a writer, editor, lifelong teacher of writing, former college admissions director, and college counselor, I have lived and breathed what I have written about in these pages.

Writing did not always come easy to me. I remember many tortured nights in high school trying to crank out English essays. I would begin at the beginning as all good writing students are taught to do—after all, you need an introduction, don't you?—and get all tangled up before I even got started.

Hamlet, the main character of Shakespeare's play of the same name…No, no, no! Shakespeare's play *Hamlet*, whose main character, Hamlet…The main character of Shakespeare's play *Hamlet*, Hamlet…

Sound familiar?

I remember crumpling up paper after paper—this was before there were computers—and wanting to give up.

In fact, if, unlike Harry Potter, I had not found the power to vanquish the Dark Lord of Writer's Blo*#k (whose name must not be spoken), I would have been interpreting CT scans and performing brain surgery. That was the life I was headed for—I was a premed English/Biology double major devouring romantic poetry and going through the motions of a course in neuroscience—all because of *that which shall not be named!*

Face-to-face, day after day, with the blank page, I was at my wit's end.

Then, one day, I discovered what I'm going to teach you.

And it changed my life—literally.

Not only did I *not* become a doctor, I became a writer—and a teacher of writing, at that!

I am sure my own journey has helped me help others learn to write. From years of painful experience, I know firsthand what it is to suffer from *that which shall not be named.*

The dark forces are powerful, but with the right kind of wizardry, they can be completely disarmed.

I could have called this book *Ten Easy Steps to a Winning College Essay* or *How to Write the Best Essay of Your Life* (which I certainly hope this book will help you do). But instead, I called it *The ART of the College Essay* because writing is an art—but no one really talks about the "art" of it. Everyone tells you what your final product should contain: A story. A clever, catchy opening. A twist or surprise. Specific detail. Showing and not telling. And it should start in the middle.

The middle of what? And how do you *do* these things? Where do they come from? Do they just materialize out of thin air?

It is the ART—that element that is seemingly unteachable, untamable, unnameable, mysterious—that I want to address.

"The most beautiful experience we can have," Einstein said, "is the mysterious—the fundamental emotion which stands at the cradle of true art and true science."

> **Insofar as writing is an art, as with any art,**
> **one must abandon all preconceptions and be**
> **willing to step into the unknown.**

Creativity takes courage.

Thirty years of experience have taught me that there is no right way to write.

In fact, *any* way that works is a good way.

> **Experience has also taught me that there are ways to tame**
> **the inner critic and awaken the muse.**

My goal in writing this book is to get down on the page what it is I do every day that helps students write extraordinary essays out of the seeming ordinariness of their lives, that frees them from internal and external constraints, that lifts their anxiety, and introduces them, through the back door, to the writer within themselves and, ultimately, gives them tools for writing that will serve them for the rest of their lives.

Having led thousands of students on this most wonderful journey, I thought it might be a good idea to record some of my observations, map the various terrains one can come upon, and pass on some tools for navigating what really is the single most important writing journey of any student's life.

I have tried to make this a short book and one that's easy to navigate.

I hope it is fun to read.

And if I have succeeded, I will do what I'm talking about. To that end, I have often opted for anecdote over, or alongside of, explanation. In the lingo of creative writing teachers—I have tried to *show* what I am telling.

Finally, much as I want to offer reflections on the deeper aspects of the art of writing a winning essay, I hope this book will be as practical, helpful, and precise as, say, a step-by-step guide on How to Change Your Oil.

Who Is This Book Written For?

College-bound juniors and seniors, of course!

And whoever is helping them write their college admissions essays—their English teachers, college and guidance counselors, independent college counselors, and parents.

Although I've written it for this audience in particular, there's really no reason anyone who is called upon to express him or herself in writing couldn't also find it useful.

And these days, because of the Internet, that's pretty much everyone.

Not since the invention of the printing press has there been such an explosion, such a proliferation of the written word. Emailing, Facebooking, texting. Everybody is doing it!

Before Gutenberg, there were scribes, a select few who copied the works of the great masters. The Bible. *The Book of Kells.* Illustrated manuscripts. Everything was in limited edition. And very few people knew how to read and write. The printing press changed all that.

So it is with the advent of the Internet and mobile technology.

Now? My Russian grandmother, if she were still alive, God bless her, would be texting to remind me to button up my jacket when it gets cold and to "pick up some lamb chops, while you're at it, on your way home."

The written word is no longer a rare commodity. It's like air. It's everywhere. We're literally bathed in it.

Have the Internet and mobile technology changed the way we communicate? Of course they have. How could they not?

From a commentary in *Digital Trends:*

> Certain acronyms, neologisms, and abbreviations have infiltrated everyday speech—if I say something like "OMG, why did my ex like my status, obvi I'm unfriending him," most people would know what I'm talking about (even if they'll roll their eyes at how annoying I am). Since people often communicate online and through text messages, truncated turns of phrase and space-saving emoticons are now mainstream.
>
> http://www.digitaltrends.com/social-media/how-the-internet-is-changing-the-way-we-talk/#ixzz2pS5K3oPS

Internet-speak has infiltrated our language. There's no getting around it.

Recently, a student asked if it would be appropriate to use ;-), a wink emoticon, in his college essay.

Perfectly placed, at the right moment, with intentionality, in an intelligent, well-expressed essay—why not?

Personally, I think it would be very twentieth century of me to categorically say no. ;-)

But there are drawbacks to the ubiquity of the written word.

When I was growing up, you picked up the phone to call a friend. Now, when you want to communicate with a friend, you DON'T pick up the phone. Or if you do, you hope (generally speaking, that is) that whomever you're calling won't answer.

I'm sure you've had this conversation:

"Hi, Josh! Oh, I didn't expect you to pick up."

"Oh hi, Gabby, would you like me to hang up so you can call me back and leave a message?!"

Instead of calling, you shoot your friends a quick text—or an email.

So everyone is writing. And I believe everyone is capable of learning how (which is the premise of this book). But the ubiquity of the written word in modern life also means that people who have very little understanding of the rules of grammar are writing all the time, and billions of people, potentially, are reading what they've written—and believing that it's correct.

This means that grammatical "errors" are being broadcast all over the world even as we speak.

This causes a strange double standard. On one hand, students are expected to know that "due to" is *never, never* used in formal language. Pick up any SAT book, turn to the section on usage or diction, and you will see this rule.

Due to inclement weather, due to the rise in gas prices—due to the use of "due to" just about everywhere, students are using "due to," too.

So there's that.

You know how to dash off a text or an email. You may even have a formula for how to write a five-paragraph essay. But how *do* you write something that's truly important to you—a cover letter, a profile description, a *college essay*—when you are called upon to do so?

How do you write the most important essay of your life in a form (the narrative personal essay) you have probably never heard of, let alone mastered?

That's what I'm going to tell you.

How Is This Book Organized?

The first half of the book looks at what makes a good essay good, or what I call *Product*. This part will help you bring into focus what you're aiming for, what your end product (roughly) should look like or contain. Few students setting out on this journey already know where they want to go. They really have no idea what a college essay is, primarily because they've never written one. And so it is important to show them.

The second half of the book focuses on *Process*—how you get where you want to go. In this part, I outline the steps from point A to point B. It's not about *what it is*, it's about *what to do* and *how to clean up and spruce up your essay once it's written*.

Following this, there is a note to parents, a few last words on the art of the college essay, and then the appendices, which provide information such as sample prompts, a quick reference guide, and a list of pithy adjectives I thought would be helpful to have at your fingertips.

A Note on Product and Process

> *How you write* your college essay (Process) and *what it looks like once it's written* (Product) are often confused, **but they are not the same.**

I want to pause for a moment to speak about the differences between the two.

Knowing where you want to end up before you set off on your journey is crucial. Otherwise, you would be out there wandering in the woods. But seeing the destination pinpointed on a map and looking at pictures of the place you want to go do not tell you anything about how to get there.

Even in the case of the five-paragraph essay—I'm sure you're intimate with those—probably no one ever actually taught you *how* to do it (Process). They just told you what it should look like when it was done (Product):

Your five-paragraph essay should contain five paragraphs, they said. It should begin with an introduction that houses a thesis—of course, the thesis! The thesis should be arguable and articulated in one (usually long) sentence in which you give reasons to support what will be your argument. Your three body paragraphs should each begin with a topic sentence drawn directly from your reasons (above) and should provide evidence—quotes from the text—to support your thesis. Oh yes, and your conclusion, how can we forget that? Your conclusion should add to or expand upon what you have already stated without repeating your thesis verbatim.

Sound familiar?

How do you begin? Of course, you start from the beginning! You start by writing an introduction, right? Everyone knows that.

Not.

> **Introducing something before you know what you want to say, from my perspective anyway, is a recipe for *that which shall not be named.***

(We will face off with this particular demon later in the book).

The truth is they tell you what it should look like, but they don't tell you how to get there.

But we must not blame them. No one told them.

It would seem natural, given what I've just explained, to start with Process, not Product, since presumably you're reading this book to find out *how* to do it, not what it *is*.

But, actually, I'm going to do it the other way around. I'm going to start by showing you what it is you're aiming for (Product) and then I'm going to tell you how to get there (Process). As long as you don't confuse the two, you'll be fine.

> N.B. If you already know what you're aiming for—and are clear about the differences between Product and Process—you can go straight to Part II of this book [Process]. Process is where I often begin when working with a student. After he or she has identified "moments" on which they will Free Write, I show them models and speak about the form in which we are working—the narrative essay—as the need for this information arises. There's a lot of useful information in Part I, but the book does not necessarily need to be read in order, as I will explain in the next section.

How Do You Use This Book Most Effectively?

This book can be used either as a trouble-shooting guide, a quick how-to, or a journey in and of itself.

Who you are and where you are in the process of writing your college essay will dictate which way works best for you.

For a quick step-by-step guide (indexed in case you need more detail), you can go straight to Appendix C.

Or, you can skim the book and just read the tips, which I have highlighted in gray.

If you are stuck, don't know where to begin, or are in the middle of your essay and don't know what to do next, the Trouble-Shooting Guide in Appendix E would be the place to go. Here I have listed questions with page numbers (or links) so you can go back to any section you want, immediately, and find whatever piece of advice you're looking for.

And finally, if—as when the Ad Com reads a winning college essay—you are drawn to read this book from beginning to end, all the better. My hope then would be that the journey offers you more than you could have predicted when you set out on it.

To sum up: You can use this book in one of three ways (or any other way you like):

1. You can read it from start to finish.

2. You can start at Part III (Process) and take it from there.

3. You can go directly to Steps to Writing a Winning College Essay (Appendix C).

4. You can go to the Trouble-Shooting Guide with specific questions.

Or any combination thereof.

I'd love your feedback, by the way, if you'd like to give it to me, on how the book worked best for you.

PART II

Product

1. Oh, the Places You Can Go!

> Immature poets imitate; mature poets steal; bad poets deface what they take, and good poets make it into something better, or at least something different.
>
> —T.S. Eliot, The Sacred Wood

> An original writer is not one who imitates nobody, but one whom nobody can imitate.
>
> —Dan Vyleta

> Through others we become ourselves.
>
> —Lev S. Vygotsky

It would be naive to think that one learns to write in a vacuum.

One doesn't learn to speak in a vacuum. In fact, one needs to imitate in order to learn. Imitation is the highest form of praise—and one of the greatest and most underutilized tools for learning.

As a young New York City Poet-in-the-Schools, I remember being taught by the great poet Kenneth Koch how to teach students who had never written poetry to write poems.

Koch was well known for using the beginning of famous poems as starting points for young writers. He would read a poem aloud, say, "The Red Wheelbarrow" by William Carlos Williams:

so much depends
upon

a red wheel
barrow...

and then direct an entire class to start a poem with the words "so much depends upon..."

Despite beginning with the exact same words, each student's poem was unique. True, they all started out the same, but where they went was completely different. Here is another example, with a different prompt. Using "The Tyger" by William Blake as a model, Koch asked his students "to write a poem in which [you are] asking questions of a mysterious and beautiful creature." Here is one of the poems a student wrote in response to this prompt.

Dog, where did you get that bark?

Dragon, where did you get that fire?

Kitten, where did you get that meow?

Rose, where did you get that red?

Bird, where did you get those wings?

Koch even used the bolded line of this poem as a title for his book on using models to teach students how to write.

What Koch also taught, using "The Red Wheelbarrow" specifically, is that in writing, as in life, really, so much depends on so little.

The words we use every day were already in circulation when we got here. No one has cornered the market on language.

The old masters—da Vinci, Michelangelo, Rembrandt—knew well that imitating the great masters who came before them was the way to go.

**The irony of the college essay is that
students are asked to write the best
essay of their lives in a form
they have never learned.**

Maybe a student has read a few personal essays in his or her high school career. Maybe essays by Annie Dillard or Richard Rodriguez.

Perhaps he or she has been asked to write a "reflection" on something he or she has read in class.

But I would put money on the likelihood that no one has really taught the student to write a personal essay.

To be honest, if students were being taught how to do this, I would be out of a job!

Most students don't even really know what a personal essay is.

So it's good to show them.

I have a few favorites that I use to demonstrate the breadth and scope of what's possible—in terms of both subject matter and style.

I am always amazed at my students' responses to the model essays I read to them.

"Wow," they often say. "I didn't know you could write about that!"

Or, "That's pretty wild! Did so-and-so get in?"

I like to show them that the field is not only large but infinite, so they can play in it and find a path that is truly their own.

I usually share these models early in the process. Maybe not the first session, but close to it. I don't want students to be too swayed by reading these and find themselves unable to come up with their own ideas, but I *do* want them to know all the many (read: infinite) forms a college essay may take. So I show them some particularly unique ones.

The truth is, college essays can be about almost anything.

Speaking of which, in almost every single book that I have read about how to write college essays, the author speaks about what subjects *not* to write about. Divorce, death, and disease are some of the supposed no-no's.

But, actually, I have seen beautiful—and successful (meaning the student got in)—essays on *all* of these subjects. I have even seen a great essay about *both* divorce and disease. (The student who wrote it got into West Point.)

Writing from your heart, in your own voice, about what you're moved to write about is the way to go.

If that happens to touch on one of the above-mentioned topics, I say, "So be it."

One of my all-time favorite college essays, excerpted below, extols the virtues of the paperclip!

"You can write your college essay about a paperclip?"

You sure can, especially if it is as well written as this one is and if it reveals as much about you as this one does about the student who wrote it.

Here is the opening of "A New World Order" by Cat Hill (she got into USC early decision with this essay):

> One miraculous day, I discovered the paperclip. It was the beginning of a new world order for me. I had begun the summer naively filing my college applications into one single eight-and-a-half-by-eleven manila folder. I thought, "Great. I'll just stuff everything in here." This method worked for about a week. That is, until multiple drafts of essays tangled themselves between pages of applications and the "folder" no longer folded at a single crease. In fact, the folder had

become one big crease, losing its rectangular shape completely. It was such mayhem that I would lose items inside the folder for weeks at a time until, as if by some miracle, they would suddenly reappear. Then the day came. I discovered the seemingly simple, twisted world of adult organization. How delicately those metallic tendrils of angel hair clasped to my stacks of papers. My discovery of the paperclip inspired me to invent the "sub-section," where essays could rest within categories in my dilapidated manila folder. That curled strand of genius initiated the beginning of a whole new era in my life—The Era of Organization!"

Even though the subject of this essay seems to be the virtues of the paperclip, actually it's about a lot more than that. What do you learn about the writer from reading this essay or even an excerpt of this essay?

You can see this writer is a risk-taker (writing your college essay about a paperclip?), creative, a good writer, honest (she's not afraid to describe the error of her ways *before* she sees the light and becomes organized.) Clearly, she is intelligent and has a good sense of humor. You can be sure the Ad Com read this essay from beginning to end—which is saying *a lot*. Ultimately, as I mentioned in the introduction, that is the final test of whether an essay does or does not do what it's supposed to—help you get into college.

Here's another essay. This one is a response to the following prompt: "Describe a place or environment where you are perfectly content. What do you do or experience there, and why is it meaningful to you?"

I am secretly a mermaid, a mythical goddess of the sea, singing my alluring song. The ocean flows through my veins and nature is my mother. I am one with the water, the currents, and the tides. I breathe in the saltiness of the sea and the crispness of the air. I dive and twirl, gazing up at the surface and see beams of sunlight penetrating the speckled density, shining sparkling rays down into the abyss. The deep green kelp sways with the rhythm of the tides, dancing back and forth. The water is cool, enlivening. When I dive deeper, through spiraling threads of light, I enter a bright kind of darkness. Here there is a silence that consumes me. Although it is silent, I hear something. But what I hear is not a true sound. It is a calling from within.

The blinding walls of concrete, the chaos of responsibility, the tainted air, the traffic of everyday life—sirens, horns, carbon dioxide, famine, cancer, crime, scandal, lies, even everyday boredom or anxiety or frustration. Down here, none of that exists.

I glide through the depths. Cool water slides like silk across my tail. Freedom. I am happiest here. Entering my kingdom, I open doors to the other world: a new way of thinking, a new way of life. Underwater, I escape gravity through the miracle of buoyancy, which undoes the constraints of mass and pull and allows me to let go. In the water, everything dissolves except for the particles of, what are they? Remnants of song? Memories?

But this is not forever. I live in two worlds, not one. I must return to land; it is half of who I am. I must emerge and shake the water off my tail, for I am not a fish, I am a mermaid. For a moment, the air feels foreign and empty. I feel a strange lightness and an uncomfortable ease of movement. Everything is too fast. But that, too, is who I am. And so I see the contrast, which is my magnifying glass to the wonder and greatness of the sea. Like the ebb and flow of the tides, the time will always come for me to return. But wherever I go, I take the water with me. With a flick of my tail, I go down to the heavens I call home. Down into the depths of water I dive, where I am renewed, moved by the tides, captivated by the feeling.

This essay got Morgan Hankamer into Notre Dame.

By the way, prompts are simply the questions colleges ask that you are answering in your college essay. Although the phrasing of prompts may vary, basically colleges want to know:

- Who are you?

- How do you think?

- How do you learn?

- How do you adapt to change (ever-present in real life) and deal with adversity (ever-present in real life)?

- What's important to you?

- What are your prospects for success in the future?

- Can you write?

- Are you a good fit for our school?

Sophia Held wrote the essays that follow. She got into every college she applied to and chose UCLA for its major in screenwriting.

The first essay, "On Fog," is also a response to the Common App prompt number four—describe the place you feel most at home.

> … the way it draws me in from afar, appearing to me as a cloud that has fallen onto the earth. It moves slowly around the hills, wraps itself around them like a ribbon.
>
> In the fog, there is no distraction. Looking down there is grey, looking up there is grey, and it is impossible to see the lines between the earth, the sky, and the sea. In the fog I become grey. I am my surroundings and my surroundings are me. I feel at ease; I feel whole. I feel found and yet the fog has gotten me lost.
>
> Growing up in San Francisco, fog has become a character in the story of my life. In the foggy times, it is the one thing I can count on. In the good times, it reminds me to stay in the moment because I can only see what lies right in front of me.
>
> It's there and it's not.
>
> Where does it come from?

This one was in response to the University of California's "My World" question: "Describe the world you come from—family, school, community—and how it has shaped your dreams and aspirations."

> I write my world and my world writes me.
>
> Neither of my parents received easy opportunities. My father grew up in the ghettos of New York City, where society labeled him a hoodlum and threw him into the heap of unremarkable teenagers destined to grow old working at their father's plumbing companies. With no education but a lot of guts and drive, my father left Long Beach, New York in 1964. He went to Wall Street where he begged Lehman Brothers Holding to take a chance on him. When given this amazing opportunity, he did not let it slip away. He worked tirelessly to prove

himself, often staying in the building long after all his colleagues had gone home, and in 1971, my father became the top seller on Wall Street.

Upon my mother's graduation from high school, she was given two options: get married or go to secretarial school. The day after she graduated from high school, she took the train into New York City and began going door-to-door at modeling agencies. My mother is a beautiful woman with a "snaggle tooth" and a gap in between her two front teeth. This often meant her polite smile was received with a door slamming in her face. Where most people would have quit, my mother worked harder. She began revisiting agencies that had already turned her away, taking each rejection as motivation to work even harder. The third time she found herself sitting in the waiting room at Wilhelmina Modeling Agency, something amazing happened. Right as the receptionist began to recite the familiar speech about my mother's teeth, Wilhelmina Cooper herself walked into the waiting room, pointed a finger at my mother and said, "Give her a chance." My mother's positive attitude and *je ne sais quoi* set her apart from all the pretty faces, and in 1979, she was named cover girl for Estee Lauder.

I want to be a writer. I know my path will be no less difficult than that of my parents, but they have given me the gift of motivation. Through example, they have shown me what it takes to succeed. They have also given me plenty to write about! ;-)

As you can see, Sophia Held used a wink emoticon at the end of her essay.

This next essay was in response to the question: "Why NYU?" The "Whys" are really difficult. I always have students write these essays last, so they don't get hung up on them before answering the longer, more involved questions. But Sophia did an amazing job here.

My heart beats louder than it should. In an X-ray it is invisible but I can feel it every day. It is the fast-paced intense rhythm that is the soundtrack for my life, the physical manifestation of the motivation that pushes me forward. My heart beats too loud for safe, suburban Marin where I live; it is too intense for an ivy-covered hideaway in the Midwest; my heart belongs in New York City!

I am absolutely enamored with words. It's sometimes scary to turn my back on all the safe occupations I have been told I should pursue, but I want to do what makes me happy. Every day on my way to school as I drive across the Golden Gate Bridge I am writing stories in my head, and more often than not, I am completely intrigued by the juxtaposition of what is going on in my head and what is going on around me. Against the fog-covered ocean and soft green headlands, the words come alive. I want the world to read what I have to say and I believe NYU is the place to cultivate my talent.

I live my life fast. I am constantly moving towards a goal and don't like to waste a minute of my day waiting around. I am drawn to NYU for its atmosphere of creativity, opportunity and vibrant *joie de vivre*. NYU has a heartbeat. And it is loud, just like mine.

Below is an essay by a student who got in early decision to Williams. This essay pulls together three distinct moments from his life, which, it turned out, all had a common theme:

I looked down the lake and saw the lit street lamp that I would steer towards; the sun was just starting to crest over the horizon as our coach gave us the command to start. My JV eight was doing full practice races or "race pieces," as we called them, against the varsity eight. They were bigger, stronger and faster, but on that cold morning, we had heart, and we won, not because we were the best but because we wanted it the most. Jeff, one of my former coaches, used to scream *carpe diem* at us through his megaphone as his face turned red. That morning, my teammates and I seized the day. Part of my job during a race is to sense when the time is right to make a move, when we should spring, and when we should hold back to conserve our energy. There is a risk that I might be wrong—we might make our move and it won't work at all and we'll have wasted our energy at the wrong time. It's my job to make that decision—to seize the right moment and make the call—and this is one of the main reasons I love crew.

Three summers ago, during a crew exchange with rowers in Germany, I had the opportunity to visit Dachau, one of the five concentration camps my grandfather survived. One of the rowers on the trip who was also Jewish broke down when we looked at the sign over the barracks that read, *Arbeit Wird Sie Befreien Setzen* (Work Will Set You Free). At that moment, I thought about my grandfather whom I greatly admire.

I wondered whether he cried the first time he saw that sign or at times when he thought he might die. My grandfather made it out of the camps to safety by jumping off a speeding train that would have brought him to his death. When my grandfather jumped off the train, he took the opportunity that was given to him; he didn't wait around to die. My grandfather didn't survive purely because he was lucky—though luck did play a part. He survived because he wanted to and he took risks.

Two summers ago, we took a family trip to Kenya and visited a Maasai village on the north side of the The Maasai-Mara National Reserve. We gave the leader of the village money to enter. We were told they spend the money they receive from tourists to send their children away to school to start a new, westernized life. I found it ironic that our presence was facilitating their cultural destruction. Would the educated Maasai children walk around Nairobi in their elaborate beadwork and blood red skirts? At first I was disappointed at what seemed like the loss of the Maasai way of life. Then I realized that just like my grandfather, the Maasai had been granted a golden opportunity and they took it.

In order to take full advantage of an opportunity, one must first see that there is one. For reasons I don't quite understand—perhaps it is in my blood—I have this ability. Having to make snap decisions that count is what I thrive on. For this reason, and because I want to dedicate my life to helping others, I want to be a surgeon.

The essay that follows, which I had lost—and found again on the Internet by googling "Crazy college essay that got student into NYU" was written by Hugh Gallagher:

I am a dynamic figure, often seen scaling walls and crushing ice. I have been known to remodel train stations on my lunch breaks, making them more efficient in the area of heat retention. I translate ethnic slurs for Cuban refugees, I write award-winning operas, I manage time efficiently.

Occasionally, I tread water for three days in a row.

I woo women with my sensuous and godlike trombone playing, I can pilot bicycles up severe inclines with unflagging speed, and I cook

Thirty-Minute Brownies in twenty minutes. I am an expert in stucco, a veteran in love, and an outlaw in Peru.

Using only a hoe and a large glass of water, I once single-handedly defended a small village in the Amazon Basin from a horde of ferocious army ants.

I play bluegrass cello, I was scouted by the Mets, I am the subject of numerous documentaries. When I'm bored, I build suspension bridges in my yard. I enjoy urban hang gliding. On Wednesdays, after school, I repair electrical appliances free of charge.

I am an abstract artist, a concrete analyst, and a ruthless bookie. Critics worldwide swoon over my original line of corduroy evening wear. I don't perspire. I am a private citizen, yet I receive fan mail. I have been caller 'number nine' and have won the weekend passes. Last summer I toured New Jersey with a traveling centrifugal-force demonstration. I bat .400.

My deft floral arrangements have earned me fame in international botany circles. Children trust me.

I can hurl tennis rackets at small moving objects with deadly accuracy. I once read *Paradise Lost, Moby Dick,* and *David Copperfield* in one day and still had time to refurbish an entire dining room that evening. I know the exact location of every food item in the supermarket. I have performed several covert operations for the CIA. I sleep once a week; when I do sleep, I sleep in a chair. While on vacation in Canada, I successfully negotiated with a group of terrorists who had seized a small bakery. The laws of physics do not apply to me.

I balance, I weave, I dodge, I frolic, and my bills are all paid. On weekends, to let off steam, I participate in full-contact origami. Years ago I discovered the meaning of life but forgot to write it down. I have made extraordinary four course meals using only a mouli and a toaster oven.

I breed prizewinning clams. I have won bullfights in San Juan, cliff-diving competitions in Sri Lanka, and spelling bees at the Kremlin. I have played Hamlet, I have performed open-heart surgery, and I have spoken with Elvis.

But I have not yet gone to college.

What can we see about him from this essay?

Clearly, he has a sense of humor. He also seems to possess a very broad understanding of how the world works, of cultures and their particularities. He knows what a covert operation is and that there is such a thing as a mouli used for cooking. He has a sense of humor, a lighthearted spirit, upstanding values ("Children trust me").

He has high aspirations, is creative, bold, inventive, articulate—and, let's face it, the guy knows how to write!

Would you accept him into your college even if his grade point average were only a 3.3? I probably would.

The real point, however, is "Oh the places you can go" in your essay. They are infinite and await you.

For more sample essays, you can look in Appendix E in the back of this book. You can also find some wonderful essays in Best College Essays 2014. Here is the link for that book: http://www.amazon.com/Best-College-Essays-2014-Volume/dp/0991214900

2. Why Not Just Say It Directly?

So, you wanna know who I am and why you should accept me at your school in five hundred words or less? No problem! That's easy! What's all the fuss about?

Yeah, what *is* all the fuss about and *why not just say it directly?*

Joe Schmoe decided to take the bull by the horns and tell them what they wanted to know. Here is his essay. He hardly needed the allotted 650 words.

> Hi, I'm Joe Schmoe. I want to go to University X, Y, or Z, and I think you should accept me. Here are the reasons why: My grades are good. I have participated in many interesting extracurricular activities. I did well on my SATs. I've achieved a lot and as I think you can see from my essay, I'm a perfect fit for your school.

If it only worked that way! Then everyone could simply copy, cut, and paste this mini essay into his or her applications, replace Joe Schmoe's name with his or her own, and get into the school of his or her dreams.

You can't say it directly because, well, why would they believe you?

It's not about writing something you think will please the Ad Com, it's about writing something that is a true expression of *you*.

I know from sitting on the other side of the table that

colleges are looking for an essay that's deeply felt and real, that shows the writer's intelligence and sense of herself and the world, and of course, that is beautifully, impeccably, and interestingly written.

What is it that makes a great essay great?
I guess the short answer is Heart, Smarts, and Art.

Anyone who's ever worked in college admissions (as I have) or read college essays for a living (as I do) knows that a winning essay wins because it *shows* who you are without your ever having to say it.

Anyone can say he's good at chess. They want you to *show*, and by *showing*, convince them you're good at chess. And more than that, they want you to *show*—in the form of a personal, narrative essay—how you got to be good at it, why you like it, what you do when you lose, and how you've come back from those losses to become someone they want at their school.

But how do you do this?

That is where the *art* comes in.

3. What Exactly Is a Narrative Personal Statement, Anyway?

The College Essay or Personal Statement is a narrative essay about *you*.

Have you ever written a narrative essay before? Probably not. Perhaps you've written a reflection in your English class—a paragraph or two on how you *feel* about something you've read.

But a full-fledged narrative essay upon which your entire future hinges?

First of all, what is a narrative?

A narrative is a story such as you would read in a novel.

And given the fact that you're only allotted 500 to 600 words to tell your story, your story's got to be short.

Why don't they call it a short story, then?

For one thing, because it's supposed to be truth (whatever that is) and not fiction.

For another, it's a narrative *essay*.

An essay is different from a short story. In addition to telling a story, an essay reflects on the story that's being told.

When you write an analytical essay for school—the five-paragraph essay we just spoke about—it's *all* reflection, but only about the subject you are analyzing—not about *you*. There's no place for an "I" in a traditional analytical essay.

In a narrative essay, you tell a story that embodies/illustrates/reveals/*shows who you are*—and then

> **you reflect on the story you've just told
> —which shows *how you think.***

Your English teacher or college counselor may already have quoted you the rule of thumb everyone tells everyone when they are writing college essays—*Show, Don't Tell.*

In a narrative essay, however, you have to do *both*—tell a story *and* reflect on it.

> **A more accurate rule of thumb for writing college essays
> should be Show *and* Tell!**

To do this, you must leave all the rules of the five-paragraph essay behind and embark on a journey into the unknown.

This is where the "art" comes in. The magic.

> **You must be willing to get lost in order to be found.**

In the words of Friedrich Nietzsche: "You must have chaos within you to give birth to a dancing star." We will discuss how to do this in the section on Process.

Here, in your personal statement, not only are you allowed to use "I," you must.

There is no thesis (though there may be a moral or lesson you learned).

Who knows how many paragraphs it'll turn out to be.

> **You must tell a good story. And tell it well. And
> somewhere in there, you must reflect
> on what you are telling us.**

4. Why Do Colleges Want Narrative Essays?

For one thing, there are too many applicants to interview them all. The personal statement is the closest thing the Ad Com has to an actual interview. The college essay is the place where the colleges "meet you." That is why it's so important to use this opportunity to turn two dimensions into three—to *show and tell* them what you're made of.

Secondly, they want to know how you think.

Writing is a good way to express that.

How you choose to tell your story says a lot about you.

Thirdly, writing well is important. In fact, in your academic career, it's crucial.

They want to know how you write.

Actually it doesn't really matter what question you're answering or what form you're writing in—the process is basically the same.

The reason your English or creative writing teachers or college counselors are repeating over and over S*how, Don't Tell* is that you have been so trained to tell and not show that they are trying to get you to break old habits, let your hair down, and be free. (Trying to be free? Isn't that an oxymoron?)

But, as we said, you are misled if you think you must only *show*, for telling is crucial, too.

So, the college essay is a personal essay that is narrative. It is made up of little stories and reflections on these stories.

We call a short, contained story an anecdote, and because the anecdote doesn't tell your whole life story, but just one incident in your life, it's a *slice of life*. A narrative essay may contain more than one anecdote, and usually does.

The anecdote is the building block of the narrative essay.

Make no mistake about it, though. If your essay were only made up of anecdotes with no reflection, it would be like bones with no muscles attached to them.

So you must have both anecdotes and reflections on these anecdotes.

OK, we've established that. Now…down to the most basic basic.

5. What Is a Story?

A story unfolds in time and space (even if the time is infinity and the space is the moon).

Can a story be frozen in time where nothing unfolds?

No. That would be a description only—the equivalent of a still life.

A story needs to progress over time.

This happens and then that happens and then this happens and so on.

A story needs a character (at least one).

In *The Great Gatsby*, the main character is the narrator, Nick, who tells the story. In *The Life of Pi*, the tiger is a character. So is the boat, the sea, and the weather!

In your college essay, *you* are the main character, even if you are writing about someone else!

Even if your essay is about your best friend, your grandfather, a teacher who had a profound effect on you, the story is about *you*—how you responded to this person, how the relationship affected/formed you, what you feel about that person.

And something must *happen*—even if what happens is nothing! ;-)

A story also needs a conflict—a problem, dilemma, or obstacle. There must be tension of some kind.

Let me illustrate:

Your best friend came over. You decided to go to the rope swing over the ravine where last year a girl in your class fell and nearly died. She hadn't wanted to jump, but felt pressure from her friends (with friends like these, who needs enemies?). Against her own better judgment, she did it anyway. She grabbed the rope and swung. Then her fear must have gotten the better of her, and she let go of the rope. It was a terrible tragedy.

Now here you are. You and your best friend go to the ravine. You're both afraid. You both jump, swing, safely return to the cliff, and go home.

End of story.

See, nothing really "big" happened—except that the actual experience proved your fear unfounded (sort of) and defied the expectations of the reader, who was expecting something bad to happen.

The conflict is: Should I or shouldn't I jump?

The tension comes from the fact that someone you know almost died doing this.

This in itself creates suspense for the reader.

6. What Do You Mean by Reflection?

In a narrative essay, you need to reflect on the experience. You need to express your thoughts and feelings about it—

how it felt, what you learned, what you think about what happened to you.

Here is one possible reflection on the story I just told you:

> If I had to do it over, I wouldn't have gone. I survived the experience, but it was really dangerous. **I realize** that I jumped for the same reason the girl who had been injured jumped—peer pressure—and *I see that's never a good reason to do anything.* **In the future, I hope** *to make a different choice.*

Reflecting on what you might do in the future is only one of many possible ways to end this story. But of course the Ad Com's ears will perk up because at the very moment they are reading this story, they are trying to decide whether you will be a character in the story of their future, and they will be a character in yours!

The story I told is completely bare bones—and it's a true story. It's an abstracted, pared-down version of a real student essay about this incident.

What I have here has the potential to be a rich and interesting story, but the way I've told it, it's like a dry branch lying on the ground, a mere skeleton—no leaves, no roots, no branches, no berries, no flowers…dead.

Again, please remember, we are still *only* looking at Product. The moment for discussing Process will come, but right now, I am trying to show you what goes into this big, meaningful essay you're supposed to write. It's fine to look at the Product, to take it apart even, to see how it works, as long as you don't mistake the Product for the Process. They are totally distinct, as I said.

7. What Makes a Great Story Great?

A poem must not mean, but be.

—Archibald MacLeish

It's all in the details—in what you put in and what you leave out—and where you choose to put what.

Here is the original essay with all the details filled in instead of left out:

Steep Ravine is a place I never want to go back to. When my best friend, Todd, suggested we ride our bikes there, I wasn't sure.

"Come on, Nick," he said.

It was a hot still August day in rural Tennessee where I live with my two brothers, my mom and my dad. There's not that much to do in the summer except sit around and say, "What do you wanna do?" "I dunno. What do you wanna do?"

"Come on, Nick," Todd said again. "We can even drive!" Todd dangled the keys to his mom's car in front of my eyes. He had just gotten his license a few weeks before.

Finally, I said, "Okay. But we might as well ride our bikes." I didn't trust Todd's driving and the tree swing we were heading for was too deep in the woods to drive to anyway.

The whole way I had this weird feeling—hot and cold at the same time. I remembered Molly's friends saying "Come on," the day she swung over the dry riverbed and let go of the rope just as Todd said to me.

We were so far in the woods there was no reception on our phones. By the time the paramedics got there, Molly had passed out.

The place was just as I remembered it. We had been swinging on that rope and jumping in the river since we were little kids. But last year, we had a drought and the riverbed was dry. The activity that was as familiar as brushing your teeth became a challenge in my group of friends, even a dare.

"I'll go first," Todd said, and he jumped on the rope swing.

Todd has this straight, shiny red-blond hair that always fell into his eyes. When he was swinging, it blew in the wind and stood straight up on his head.

"You should see your hair," I shouted.

In an instant, Todd was back on the platform next to me. His face was red and he was out of breath as if he had just run a four minute mile. His freckles even seemed to be more alive as if they were jumping off his face.

"Your turn," he said.

Suddenly, the hot and cold feeling started again.

"You scared?" he asked.

"No," I lied.

He handed me the rope.

I don't even remember what happened next. Everything was kind of warped like in slow motion—kind of blurry and also speeded up.

"Don't look down," Todd shouted.

Maybe he was remembering the same thing I was.

I didn't. I just held on and hoped the momentum of my swing would bring me back to the platform.

I would never do this again and I would tell anyone who asked me to listen to his deepest heart. I was afraid Todd would think I was a chicken. I wanted to challenge myself. I'm an athlete; I'm strong; I can do it, I thought.

Next time, I will not only look before I leap, I won't even leap, not over a dry riverbed, anyway. I'll take the risks that feel right to me. And I'll check it out with myself first. Even though I'm from a small town in Tennessee, Columbia University feels right to me. I'm scared, but it's a good kind of scared. And it's a challenge I hope you'll give me the opportunity to take.

As I mentioned, this is a real essay written by a real student. Let's go back and analyze the essay to see what makes it great. Nick got into Columbia, by the way.

So what's great about this essay?
It has a great opening line, one that makes you want to read on:

"Steep Ravine is a place I never want to go back to."

The essay starts in the middle.

In literary terms, this would be called *en medias res*. In cinematic terms: *the cold open*. It's very effective. Why? It's mysterious. The reader will naturally ask *why* or in this case, *why not*?

And so the suspense begins.

The essay doesn't just tell what happened; it *shows* what happened by using specifics, dialogue, details, similes, metaphors, and imagery.

Here are some examples of dialogue in the essay: "What do you wanna do?" "I dunno. What do you wanna do?" The writer could have used one declarative sentence instead of dialogue. He could have said: *We were bored.* The dialogue brings it to life.

The writer uses vivid description:

"His freckles even seemed to be more alive as if they were jumping off his face." This gives a sense of the adrenaline rush this act has given him.

"Todd has this straight, shiny red-blond hair that always fell into his eyes. When he was swinging, it blew in the wind and stood straight up on his head." This description makes it seems as if even his hair was expressing the excitement and tension of the moment.

Mixed into the description, dialogue, and narration, there are reflections on what is happening or what the writer is feeling:

"I didn't trust Ted's driving." I felt "hot and cold at the same time." "I would never do that again." "There's not much to do in the summer."

"Next time, I will not only look before I leap, I won't even leap, not over a dry river bed, anyway. "

The writer uses specifics: Todd, August, Steep Ravine, freckles, rural Tennessee.

He appeals to the senses: "hot and cold at the same time," warped like in slow motion.

He uses metaphors and similes:

"familiar as brushing your teeth," "as if they were jumping off his face," "as if he had just run a four minute mile."

The action unfolds over time. There is a conflict:

Should I or shouldn't I jump?

And there is a resolution:

"I would never do that again, but taking the leap to go from rural Tennessee to Columbia University is one I am ready for."

Note: "I would never do that again" ties back to the opening sentence: "Steep Ravine is a place I never want to go back to."

> **It is always good in your conclusion to bring back a thread that was introduced in the opening of the essay. It gives a sense of coherence to what you have written.**

You can track the "plot" or the incidents that unfold over time to see how it develops:

- The *now of the telling* in which he says "Steep Ravine is a place I'll never go back to."

- The recounting of past events. First, Ted suggests they go jump at Steep Ravine. He dangles the key in front of his eyes. And so on.

- The moment he decides to go with Ted.

- The moment he feels hot and cold on the way there.

- The flashback of Molly's accident.

- The moment Ted swings.

- The moment the narrator swings.

- The moment, the now of the telling, in which he reflects on the past and projects into the future.

You may not have heard the term "the now of the telling." The now of the telling is the moment in which you are writing the essay.

It is not the moment in which whatever has formed you, formed you. It is not the moment in which the action takes place when you recount a story from the past. It is now, the moment in which you are telling the story.

If you remained in the "now of the telling" for the entire essay, the essay would be a reflection only and not a story that unfolds in time. But as we have said, it needs to be both.

While you can begin an essay with the now of the telling—*I realize I am happiest when skiing*, for example—your essay will be stronger if you start in the middle of the action: *Out of nowhere, the sky opened up and it started to snow. Our teacher had just passed out our history test and I was smiling, not because I thought I would ace the test, but because I knew the next day I'd be out on the slopes.*

You can always add a reflection after the action: *I am happiest when I am skiing.*

OK, the moment we've all been waiting for!

Having taken a good look at the inner workings of a narrative essay, it is time to think about how to write one.

PART III

Process

1. What to Write About—That Is the Question— or Is It?

> Curious indeed how these things happen. The wand chooses the wizard, remember…we must expect great things from you, Mr. Potter…After all, He-Who-Must-Not-Be-Named did great things— terrible, yes, but great.
>
> —J. K. Rowling, *Harry Potter and the Sorcerer's Stone*

Students often ask, biting their nails: "What should I write about? How do I choose a topic?" And more often than not, they say, "What could I possibly have to say? Nothing big has ever happened to me."

You do need a topic. That is true. And it seems perfectly logical that you would choose a topic before you start writing, right?

My answer: Kind of. ;-) The first thing I ask students to do—after they've chosen very carefully and thoughtfully which schools are right for them—and that is the subject of another book entirely—is to gather all the prompts.

You will find a good sampling of them in Appendix A.

This is a necessary step no matter what. You need the questions to provide the answers, right? And at some point, and best done early, it's good to see that if you write an essay about such and such, for colleges X, Y and Z, you can also use it for College A, B, and Q. (Recycle wherever you can, but be careful not to get mixed up and put the name of one college on the application for another!)

But gathering the questions serves another purpose as well. One that is more profound.

Reading all these questions, the student is bathed in potentiality. I'm serious.

It's a bit scary, but also invigorating. Like jumping into icy water. Or a vigorous scrub that opens up your pores. Personally, I like to see how high the mountain is before setting out to climb it. But it's not so much even that.

The human mind is constructed in such a way that it instantaneously searches for answers whenever a question is registered.

You notice, I say when a question is registered and not just asked. I can throw a ball into the air, but it's not until you catch it that the transfer is made.

Once a question is understood, answers seem to flow naturally—and you will see this, if you pay attention.

"What are the first five things you would do if I gave you a million dollars right now?"

As soon as you comprehend what I'm asking, you will begin answering.

I can think of a thing or two myself I would do with the money if you gave me a million dollars right now!

In fact, just asking *you*, I started answering the question myself!

Your job is to catch the falling star, for that is how quick and elusive these first thoughts are.

As soon as a question is asked, jot down the first things that come to your mind. This is advice I give to students writing any essay.

First clarify the question. Put it in your own words. And then, jot down the first thoughts that come to mind, the answers that rise to the surface.

They're often good ones.

And from here, do you start writing the essay from beginning to end?

Sure, if you can. I couldn't (most of the time).

I would need to do other things first.

In fact, for me, approaching it head-on would lead to *that which shall not be named*. Even if I have some idea how I would answer the question and know what the end product is supposed to contain, I cannot simply write the essay linearly, A to Z (usually!).

**Of course, sometimes, by some miracle, one is able to write an essay from start to finish.
This is a dangerous piece of luck.**

It will give you the impression that this is how it's done. You just sit down with a question or prompt before you, and write away...Voila. Here is a finished essay. True, you do have to proofread it, but basically it's done. One try. Fantastic! That was easy.

The next time, you expect the same thing to happen. But the universe has other plans for you.

Here is an example.

Suppose the prompt is: *What is the most embarrassing thing that's ever happened to you?*

Immediately, you think of a particular moment when you were in kindergarten.

Great, you think. I have a moment. Now let me write an essay!

And so you begin:

*The most embarrassing thing that ever happened to me is when...*No, I can't say that. [False Start #1]

*I was the most embarrassed in my life when...*That's awkward. I can do better. [False Start #2:]

My sister pulled my pants down in front of my kindergarten teacher when I was six. Oh, no, I can't start the essay with that! That's the punch line. I have to lead up to it in some way. [False Start #3]

Behold the appearance of *that which shall not be named* or, in this case, what I like to call "manicuring a corpse."

> **You keep trying to get the nail polish right,**
> **but the thing is *dead*—and you're not even**
> **sure what you want to say about it.**

OK, then, what *should* I write about?

Most how-to guides tell you to choose a topic first. It makes sense, in a way. How are you supposed to write an essay if you don't know what you're going to write about?

> **I rather think, as the giver-of-wands says to Harry Potter,**
> **the wand must choose the wizard.**

But, as I said, you must take steps—and I will show you what they are—prepare the ground—to make yourself ready for the topic to find you. In the meantime, try to stay calm and take solace in the words of the great German poet, Rainer Maria Rilke:

> Be patient toward all that is unsolved in your heart and try to love the
> questions themselves, like locked rooms and like books that are written

in a foreign tongue. Do not now seek the answers, which cannot be given you because you would not be able to live them. And the point is, to live everything. Live the questions now. Perhaps you will then gradually, without noticing it, live along some distant day into the answer.

So, having gathered the prompts and looked them over, you have wandered in the field of potentiality. You have, perhaps, felt a few tugs on your line from the spirit-animals of your imagination. You have followed my advice—and jotted these down.

"The summer my mother was in jail...the time my brother convinced me to let him drive my mom's car before he got his license...the time I saw my grandfather's reflection in a mirror and thought, "I think he's going to die" and indeed, he did die later that day..."

Notice that these possible topics are really just "moments in time."

OK, so you've got some leads. What do you do with them? I would say, begin writing the heck out of whatever moves you. (I will explain more about how to do this in the section on Free Writing.)

> **I would only caution you not to be bound by your initial burst of ideas. Use these as impetuses to write, not as a prison sentence! ;-) (No pun intended!)**

In his book, *The Triggering Town*, Richard Hugo actually advises against being tethered to what he calls "the initiating subject":

> Your triggering subjects are those that ignite your need for words. When you are honest to your feelings, that triggering town chooses you. Your words used your way will generate meanings. Your obsessions lead you to your vocabulary. Your way of writing locates, even creates, your inner life. The relation of you to your language gains power. The relation of you to the triggering subject weakens.

This is a beautiful expression of how the triggering subject—that which moves you to speak/write—is only just that—a subject that triggers more thoughts, which then triggers more thoughts until you come to what you really want to write about.

Or, as William Saroyan explains, in "Starting with a Tree and Finally Getting to the Death of a Brother":

> How do you write? My answer is that I start with the trees and keep right on straight ahead...I start with these companions of place, each fixed into the soil of where it is, and sometimes the rock or rocks, and very little else, and after that the going is not only easy, it is very near rollicking.
>
> A writer writes, and if he begins by remembering a tree in the backyard, that is solely to permit him gradually to reach the piano in the parlor upon which rests the photograph of the kid brother killed in the war.

In that sense, it doesn't really matter where you start.

You can trust yourself to begin anywhere, get lost, and if you keep going, honestly allowing one thought or idea to lead to the next, you'll get where you *need* to go—not necessarily where you thought you were going.

2. If I Don't Begin with a Topic, How Do I Begin?

I remember in the fourth grade learning how to make flowcharts. Below you will find a very rudimentary, absurd kind of flowchart I made to remind you of what they are.

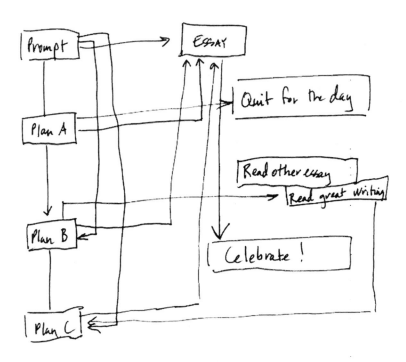

The whole idea behind a flowchart is that there is more than one means to an end.

The same goes for finding a topic.

You have to be flexible. If one path leads to a dead end, follow another.

If Plan A doesn't work, try Plan B. If Plan B doesn't work, try Plan C. And so on.

Once you have gathered all the prompts, you have a number of choices.

You can try writing an essay from beginning to end. Do it, if it comes to you, as I said. But don't expect that to happen every time.

You can look at models. That might help. But don't look too long if you think you will be too strongly influenced by what you read to think for yourself.

What I would do, and ask my students to do, is one of the following, but not necessarily in this order:

Plan A: A List of Significant Moments

Since a moment in time is what we are looking for, I like to start here. I say to the student: List five moments in your life in which you went into an experience one person or a person with one set of ideas or perspectives and came out changed—moments that changed your outlook, your feelings about yourself or the world, your perspective on life. A moment could be the length of a summer, one instant in time, a weekend, a conversation, a journey, your entire freshman year.

"What do you mean?" The student often asks.

It could be a small moment or a big one, just some moment that changed you or after which your life, or view on life, was different.

This is a very important distinction for students to make and understand. They often don't realize that something, even something small, had a major impact on them.

It is usually at this point that I begin giving examples, such as the day my teacher asked us to write down as much as we remembered of "The Star-Spangled Banner."

I wrote: "Ohhh say can you see, in the donserly light?"

"Donserly?" my teacher asked. "What's that?"

On the blackboard, she wrote, "Dawn's early light?" It turned out that I had never correctly understood the words of that song. It was a revelation. What I saw is that I could go on for a long time believing something to be true that's totally off base! This was a small moment, a few seconds only, but one I have always remembered.

Or I tell them my bear story. Strangely, or not so strangely as you will come to see, both stories have pretty much the same moral.

> We heard swearing, screaming and banging. It sounded like someone gone crazy beating a baseball bat against a garbage can. We had just drifted off to sleep.

> Suddenly, we heard a car engine very close by and bright lights shone into our tent.

> "Are you all right?" we heard a voice say.

> "We're okay," I said. "But there's some crazy guys up there," I said, pointing.

> "I don't know," the guy said. "But there's a bear."

> "I don't know about the bear," I said, "but it definitely seems like those dudes are on drugs."

> "Lady, I don't know about that," the guy in the car said again, insisting. Now *he* pointed. "But there's a bear!

> Not more than five feet away, head as big as a basketball, there stood on all fours, a very large brown bear, maybe about eight feet long, looking straight at me with his beady brown eyes.

> I was dumbfounded to say the least.

> The bear looked at me. I looked at the bear. I could see its breath in the cool night air. I must have been holding mine.

> I had believed my own story so stubbornly that I failed to see the bear right in front of my eyes!

I have often thought my bear story would be a great subject for a college essay.

I use it as an example of a "moment" in which you go into an experience one person and come out someone different on the other side—or at least with a new perspective.

My bear story is what I would consider a small incident with a big impact—a change in a long-held perspective (in my case, that I am almost always right!). You can also, of course, write about a *big* incident with a big impact. But no one is very interested in a small moment with a small impact. And, least of all, in a small moment written as if it's a big moment with a small impact. In fact, this is something strongly to avoid.

Generally speaking, the more important and profound the event, the more understated it should be. But, in some cases, for a comic effect, the reverse can be true. Taking something trivial and overdramatizing it, especially if it reveals your vulnerability, can be very funny. Cat Hill's essay about the paperclip is an example.

Your essay does not need to be about a monumental event. In fact, something mundane and everyday, if it has significance to you, can make a great subject for an essay.

Again, the essay about the discovery of the paperclip is a good example. But how do you find this experience? And what do you do when you find it? Don't worry about that yet. If you follow the steps I outline below, your topic will find you.

After I give examples from my own experience of moments in which I learned something or changed in some way—I say something like:

"Don't think about it too much! Use bullet points. Just jot down five moments in your life. Then I'll ask you to explain them to me."

The student sometimes struggles for a moment here, but generally, can come up with at least three. I'm OK with that. Three is just fine.

Once the student has the moments, I ask him or her to tell me about them. "Give me the gist," I say. I don't want them to say too much right then and there. I want them simply to fill it out a little, to sketch the outline of the horse, as it were.

The bullet points usually begin something like this: *The time* I went to my friend's house without telling my mom. *The time* I got lost in downtown San Francisco. *The time* I decided to quit tennis and regretted it.

Once the student has moments, he or she can begin writing.

Plan B: Play the Five-Adjective Game:

If Plan A worked, I go straight to The Free Write™ explained in Chapter 4, as you may do if you already have a list of significant moments.

However, if you still need more help in coming upon these moments, you can move on to Plan B.

My directions then are as follows: "Tear a piece of notebook paper in half," I say. "List five adjectives, as different from each other as you can think of, that best describe you. And I will do the same." I cover my paper playfully implying that I'm afraid the student will cheat and copy my adjectives. Before we begin, I reiterate, "Don't say, Kind, Sweet, Compassionate, Gentle and Nice. They're all basically the same. Think of five adjectives as broadly different—with my right hand I separate the outstretched fingers of my left—as you can. OK. Let's do it!"

I do the exercise simultaneously. I write about the student, of course, and not myself! Although sometimes, with very shy students, I will do the reverse and have both of us write about both of us to see whether we come up with the same or similar adjectives, and then I turn the spotlight on them. Usually I can "feel" what a student is like pretty quickly. Certainly by the time we get to this point in our work, I have a good sense. Not that it matters. What matters is that the student, himself or herself, is reflecting, perhaps for the first time in his or her life about who he or she is.

"What's an adjective again?" some students will ask. I remind them that an adjective describes a noun such as *absentminded* aardvark or *brilliant* bear.

And sometimes, if they're really stuck, I direct them to a ridiculously extensive adjective list I have compiled over the years. (See Appendix B)

If a student is really struggling to find a specific moment, I might go back and have them write a brief incident that illustrates each of their five adjectives.

"What do you mean?" they often say. I use myself as an example because, of course, I don't yet know which incidents in the student's life reflect which qualities.

Say the adjectives I wrote for myself were: Driven, Funny (I certainly think so), Reliable and Visionary (if I may say so myself ;-)). I am also Impatient, Impulsive and sometimes Silly. It's fine to use "negative" characteristics as long as you are on the road to overcoming them and have experiences to prove it. (I'm still working on overcoming mine!)

In fact, being open about your flaws and showing how you've overcome them can be very compelling. You want to be likeable, but you don't need to be perfect.

For each quality or characteristic, represented by an adjective, I think of a moment in my life that illustrates one of these qualities, and I write an encapsulated sentence beginning with "the time I…" to express it.

How do you "illustrate" a quality or adjective?

This is a very important question and a crossroads.

Often, just by asking the students the following questions, I lead them to happen upon moments that illustrate the qualities about which they are speaking:

- How did you get like that?

- Have you always been that way?

- Has that quality in you progressed over time; has it evolved or changed? For example: "I used to be shy, but now I'm outgoing, even exuberant. My summer collaborating with other students as interested as I am in designing prosthetic limbs at Rockefeller University was the first time I started to really have fun working and interacting with others. I'm an only child. I have always been very inward and quiet. After that experience..."

- How do you exhibit that quality? Find a moment in which, without ever using the adjective to describe the quality, it will be clear to the reader that you possess it.

- Find an incident or moment in your life in which one of your qualities has been tested. "Twenty-six days without toilets, running water, electricity, or electronics, out in the wilderness with sixty pounds on my back, I saw that my love of nature..."

The true test of good writing, as we have seen, is that the person reading it can see that you're inventive, gutsy, clever, silly, or trustworthy without your ever having to use the word (adjective) itself.

This is a good place to note that it's useful to play the Five-Adjective Game, after the fact, in reverse. By this I mean, once you have completed an essay, you can ask someone else to see if he or she can come up with five adjectives that describe you, just from what you wrote. Don't worry if the adjectives they find are not the same ones you chose for yourself. You want the adjectives to be broadly based, to represent the complex set of qualities that go into making you, you.

Ascribing a moment to my adjectives, I might write:

Driven—The time I pestered and pestered my mom, who was down with the flu, to get me ice skates so I could go to Turkey Swamp Park to skate with David Gittleman, the love of my teenage life. I was about twelve. My mom understood how important this was to me, got out of bed, and got me skates, but she was mad and resentful and got sicker because of it, and I felt bad about it for my whole life even till now when I'm telling this story to you!

Creative—I'm always building, designing, writing something *all the time.* I'm in the process now of building my third house and, well, writing this book!

Funny—I love to tell stories that make people laugh. One of my favorites is about the time I was buying a teddy bear for my niece and couldn't make up my mind as to which bear to buy. I lifted one bear after another, rubbed it against my cheek to see how soft its fur was, hemmed and hawed, put it back, picked up another. Finally, a woman standing next to me in the teddy bear section of this little toy store turned to me and said, "Is it a boy or a girl?"

"I don't know," I said to the lady. I turned the teddy bear over to check! "How do you tell?"

You will notice that articulating your qualities is not enough.

That would be similar to what Joe Schmoe did in his essay.

> **You need to attach the quality to a moment in space and time so that you can tell a story that will illustrate it. Finding "moments" is really what it's all about. Using adjectives to do so is only one way to get there.**
>
> **Because, remember, life is made of moments, not qualities**

And stories are made of moments, not analysis. Some moments make a bigger impression on us than others. Sometimes, we know, even when something is happening, right at the moment it is happening, that we are creating, right here and now, a memory we will not forget.

Falling in love is like this.

Having a revelation is like this.

Any moment can be a moment we remember. It would be difficult to say why some moments are more memorable than others, or, rather, why we remember some moments more than others (Who decides which are or are not memorable, anyway?), or what ingredients go into moments that are made into memories, but it doesn't really matter. That would be the work of neuroscience. And actually, even neuroscientists will probably never explain this completely. That's the beauty and mystery of human consciousness.

By now, hopefully, you will have thought of moments. This does not necessarily mean you have a final topic—but that's fine.

A moment is enough to begin.

Once you have a "moment," you can begin a Free Write. Again, refer to the section on free writing for tips on how to do this.

Plan C: The Interview

Sometimes, *that which shall not be named* kicks in at the starting gate. No need to panic. As I said, there's more than one way to skin a cat! (That's such a gross saying. Where did that come from anyway?)

Sometimes when all else fails, I ask questions.

Because the process of writing a personal statement is personal, it involves me getting to know the student and the student getting to know him or herself. I ask questions. The student answers. I write down whatever he or she says.

If you are a student reading this, you can interview yourself, but it's always easier if someone else interviews you because speaking is different from writing. It's more spontaneous and less mediated. And, in this way, it's easier. It's also helpful if someone else is doing the writing. That way you can speak freely and leave the job of recording what you say to someone else.

You can always ask a friend to help and interview each other. But if none of these is an option, it's also fine to interview yourself.

Start with something you love to do or somewhere you love to be. Ask yourself: Why? When did I start loving that? How do I feel when I do it? Can I think of one moment in which I was happy doing A, B, or C? Can you describe that moment?

"What do you mean *describe that moment?*" students often ask.

Where were you?

When was this?

Who were you with?

What were you doing?

How did you feel?

What was important to you about that moment?

Why do you think you remember it?

The W's are a good way to fill out what you've already started writing.

I wouldn't start with them, but I would use them as a tool.

This is a great time to pause and review what we have just gone over.

In order to avoid *that which shall not be named* and because it's virtually impossible to write a great essay from start to finish, you need to prepare the ground and walk around in it before you write.

The steps are as follows:

1. Take a look at the prompts. See what they're asking.

2. Jot down first thoughts if you have them.

3. List five significant moments in your life—*the time when...the day I...I remember when*....Once you have a moment, you can skip to Chapter 4. Otherwise...

4. Play the Five-Adjective Game.

5. Interview yourself or have someone interview you.

I want to elaborate a bit more on the process of interviewing.

When I interview a student, I write everything down verbatim. Lately, by the way, I have been doing this on Skype chat or instant messaging, sometimes even when the student is right in front of me! I find it works best not to let the student speak. Every time he or she tries, I say "Write it down!" It looks like this:

So you play baseball. Do you like it?
Yes.
How long have you been playing?
Since I was five.
That's young. Did you play Little League?
No, I played on the streets.
With your friends?
No, with my dad.
He took you out to play baseball?
Yes.
How did you get so good?
In Mexico, we used these rolled up socks that were stuck together with cement-like glue. They were really hard, harder than baseballs here.
Oh, when did you go to Mexico?
I lived in Mexico for a few years.
Oh, what part?
Jalisco. Where my father is from.
And that's where you played baseball?
Yes.
Was your dad working there?

No, they took me and my brother away from my mom because she was drinking too much and getting mad all the time, so my dad took us to Mexico, to my grandmother's house, where we lived.

Oh, that sounds tough. So that's where you played baseball?

Yeah, my dad taught me everything he knew.

Oh, was he a good baseball player?

Yes, he was a catcher for the minor leagues.

Oh, I didn't know that.

From all this amazing information, it is then pretty easy to identify "moments"—life-changing moments—to write about.

"So was the topic of his essay baseball?" you might ask, eager for him to find a topic.

And my answer: You must wait and see. His topic chose him!

This is a true story, by the way.

The student also told me his mother is Japanese. The student spoke fluent Japanese and eventually moved to Japan a few years later with his mother, once she had recovered and she and his father had split up.

Just as I have done here, I wrote down everything this student said. Or transcribed it from a chat that we had on IM or Skype.

Then I turned the computer around and asked him to pick out three "moments"—discrete segments of time—that had a story attached to them.

He chose the last time he saw his mom before he was taken from her when she went on a drunken binge and broke every window in their house.

He chose the moment he arrived in Mexico and saw his paternal grandparents for the first time. He then remembered that his grandfather also played baseball and had taught his father. He remembered the smell of his grandmother's cooking.

He chose the moment he was reunited with his mom after so many years.

He then told me he used to go to Japan as a child, but when he was taken away from his mom he didn't get to go. He also wanted to write about going to Japan after not having been there for five years.

Now he is ready for the next step.

3: Preparing the Soil

You might at this point be saying, Let's get on with it. Let's write the essay, for God's sake. But as we know, if it were that easy, we would all be Joe Schmoe. You would have had no motivation to pick up this book and get this far reading it. If at any point, you feel moved to write your essay from beginning to end, by all means do it. If you want a little more advice, keep reading.

I like to use the analogy of planting a lawn.

Let's say the table or desk you are working at is your plot of ground.

Your goal is to make that patch of dry earth (on four legs), into the lushest, most beautiful lawn imaginable.

First thing you do is pull the weeds. You've got to clear it, get it ready for planting your seeds.

Next you turn over the soil; aerate it, so that the conditions are just right. Soil that is packed down too tightly makes it difficult for the little sprouts to break through.

Next, you might choose to fertilize the soil, to make it as rich as possible.

Then, when the moment is right, when the weeds have been pulled, the soil has been turned over, and it is as fertile and ready as it can be, you throw in the seeds.

The next step is to hurry up and wait. There's nothing you can do at this point, except water and check your email.

Finally, with the right combination of sun, water, and air, your little seedlings will begin to break their seed coats, push through the soil and sprout! First you see one beautiful lean blade of grass, a long one, over here toward the right. Then you see another one, shorter, but also strong, a few feet away. The next day, there are more. And then more. And more.

It is *not* time to bring in your lawn mower, much as you may be tempted (and have been taught) to do. Those poor little seedlings have hardly had a chance to sprout, and you want them all to be exactly the same height so you can have your beautiful lawn?

Don't do it!

Rather, let your seedlings grow. Let your lawn be a wild patch of unruly grass spilling over the borders.

Then, one day, when the moment is right, go get it. It's time for the lawn mower.

That's a great day. You should celebrate and invite people over. Throw a lawn-mowing party!

Preparing the soil, cultivating your ideas, and resisting the lawn mower—*this* is how you grow a beautiful, rich, green carpet of grass!

The lawn mower is the part of you that trims and cuts, edits and revises, to make everything perfect.

You should not bring it in too early or you know what will happen—*that which shall not be named!*

Pulling the weeds, turning over the soil, fertilizing the ground—these are the steps you take to make the growth possible.

No matter how you look at it, there has to be a moment of breakthrough—and then you have to let the little guys

grow. What I'm trying to say is: All roads lead to The Free Write!

I want to speak for a moment about weed pulling, soil turning, and fertilizing, just to make the elements of this extended metaphor even clearer.

How do each of these steps in growing a lawn relate to writing?

Perhaps you see it already.

Pulling Weeds: This is where you clear your desk and empty your mind of preconceptions about what you are supposed to write. Leave behind the five-paragraph essay and all that you have been told about what kind of college essay you should write.

Your essay has to come from *you*, not from who you think you should be.

Students writing college essays often feel they need to write in sophisticated language and need to be someone they are not.

Clear your mind of essay-speak and write like you talk.

It's easy to think that *who* you are and *what* you are just won't cut the mustard these days in the competitive world of college admissions. I mean after all, don't you have to be someone special to get into Stanford, Harvard, UCLA,…? (You fill in the blanks.)

The answer: You have to be you and write in your own voice.

I would like to pause for a moment to speak about *Voice*.

Voice is nothing more than the natural way you express yourself when you're not trying to be someone else.

There's no magic formula to finding your voice. You already have your voice. You just have to clear the way so that it can come out.

Writing the way you speak is a great way to do this.

So often, when I read sample essays to students about to embark on their own magical journey through the wilds of writing college essays, they say something like Noah, who is quoted in an article in *The New York Times:*

> **Noah** (with increasing defeat): **But I don't have anything to say!** I don't have some heroic family story or a liberating experience building houses in the third world. My entire family has lived in the US, and gone to college, for generations. I've never gone to bed hungry...I mean, I'm a reasonably smart, well-off kid who likes show tunes, applying to Columbia...**What part of my story hasn't been heard a thousand times?**

But in truth, all you need to be is a real person telling a real story.

No unnecessarily big words. No unnecessary drama.

Rid yourself of these ideas. They are false, and, like weeds, they will sap your True Voice.

Turning Over the Soil: This is where you breathe and relax.

The word *stream* in *stream-of-consciousness* is very important. There needs to be a flow and so there needs to be looseness.

That little seedling must first break through its own seed coat, and *then*, it must break through the soil. Think about it. That tiny, delicate, green blade of grass. It's nothing short of a miracle that it sprouts at all. Bless your apple when you eat it. It's amazing that it started out as a seed!

In writing, too, the small, still voice at the bottom of the well, your inner voice (which is what we need to call on) is very delicate and shy. Like the seedling, it needs care and tending—and it needs for the conditions to be just right.

Fertilizing: This is a very interesting step. And a very important one. Sometimes, it's not needed. The soil is already rich and ready to go.

> **The moment you are facing the possibility of *that which shall not be named*, it's good to get out your fertilizer.**

What kind of fertilizer should be used for college essays, you may ask?

And where can you get some?

To fertilize is to enrich.

To get inspiration for writing, I read.

"Reading usually precedes writing," Susan Sontag wrote in her essay, "Directions: Write, Read, Rewrite, Repeat Steps 2 and 3 as Needed." "And the impulse to write is almost always fired by reading."

As for *that which shall not be named,* if it should come up at this moment, I don't give that state of being much energy. You know the story about the grandfather who tells his grandson there are two wolves in the forest (of our souls) that are always fighting each other—the evil wolf that does not care for humanity and the compassionate wolf that wants the planet to survive.

"Which one will win?" The grandson asks.

"The one you feed," answers the grandfather wisely.

I don't want to feed the wolf that is *that which shall not be named.*

But also, there are ways out, as I mentioned at the beginning of this book.

Quitting for the day is one of them. ;-)

Try Plan B or C.

Or, fertilize the soil, thicken the plot, read great writing as inspiration.

This last tip works for me so well that I am no longer capable of reading without a pen or my computer next to me. I can hardly read a sentence anymore without being inspired to write one of my own.

If you need inspiration, read other great college essays.

I have a huge file of them. My favorites. By now, I have hundreds that I just love. And you will find some great ones in Appendix E.

Usually, just reading one or two sample essays will kick-start your engine. Reading great writing of any kind will help. Personal essays, poetry, anything super well written. I have my favorites that I use over and over again. Actually, I pick and choose depending on what I'm working on.

If I'm in the mood for experimenting with punctuation and language, I look at E.E. Cummings. Here are a few lines from his poem "somewhere i have never travelled, gladly beyond:"

> (i do not know what it is about you that closes
> and opens; only something in me understands
> the voice of your eyes is deeper than all roses)
> nobody, not even the rain, has such small hands

If I want beautiful description rich in metaphor, I go back to my favorite passages from The Great Gatsby:

> This is a valley of ashes—a fantastic farm where ashes grow like wheat into ridges and hills and grotesque gardens; where ashes take the forms of houses and chimneys and rising smoke and, finally, with a transcendent effort, of men who move dimly and already crumbling through the powdery air. Occasionally a line of gray cars crawls along an invisible track, gives out a ghastly creak, and comes to rest, and immediately the ash-gray men swarm up with leaden spades and stir up an impenetrable cloud, which screens their obscure operations from your sight.

If I want gritty, tell-it-like-it-is poetic prose, I look at *The Bell Jar* by Sylvia Plath:

> New York was bad enough. By nine in the morning the fake, country-wet freshness that somehow seeped in overnight evaporated like the tail

end of a sweet dream. Mirage-gray at the bottom of their granite canyons, the hot streets wavered in the sun, the car tops sizzled and glittered, and the dry, cindery dust blew into my eyes and down my throat.

For a matter-of-fact tone, I look at examples from Hemingway or John McPhee (a great essayist), such as these passages from the latter:

> If you free yourself from the conventional reaction to a quantity like a million years, you free yourself a bit from the boundaries of human time. And then in a way you do not live at all, but in another way you live forever.

> She has the sort of body you go to see in marble. She has golden hair. Quickly, deftly, she reaches with both hands behind her back and unclasps her top. Setting it on her lap, she swivels ninety degrees to face the towboat square. Shoulders back, cheeks high, she holds her pose without retreat. In her ample presentation there is defiance of gravity. There is no angle of repose. She is a siren and these are her songs.

For amazing descriptions of nature, I read Annie Dillard's *Pilgrim at Tinker Creek*.

> What does it feel like to be alive?

> Living, you stand under a waterfall. You leave the sleeping shore deliberately; you shed your dusty clothes, pick your barefoot way over the high, slippery rocks, hold your breath, choose your footing, and step into the waterfall...

Sometimes just reading a small passage will be enough to inspire you to put fingers to keyboard.

You can even try imitating the style of writers you like.

This is another way to use models in your writing and is often a good way to get yourself moving when you get stuck.

The first essay season after this book came out, I watched myself particularly carefully, as I guided students through the process I have described to you, to see if I do what I speak about in these pages.

Indeed, I found that I do practice what I preach, though of course, organically, not always in the order I outline in the book.

But sometimes, even following all my own advice, a student still draws a blank when asked to come up with a moment, or even to list five adjectives. Sometimes, I cannot even get a student (this is rare, but it happens) to let me interview him or her.

What do you do then?

To answer that question, I am here including a section that did not even appear in the first edition of this book because I had forgotten how resourceful one sometimes must be to get the writing process rolling.

In tough situations, or even as an added resource for students who are having difficulty breaking ground, or who are searching around for something to write, this next chapter might prove helpful.

Plan D: Wishes, Lies and Dreams

Once again, I invoke the late poet and master poet-in-the-schools, Kenneth Koch, whose book *Wishes, Lies and Dreams* has been an inspiration to so many.

Let's call the student afflicted with *that which shall not be named*, Delilah.

"Ok, Delilah," I might say. "See if you can think of a moment in time, any moment, in which you go into an experience one person and come out someone different."

"Huh?" Delilah says, looking at me as if I were an alien.

"A moment, any moment. I'm sure you have had moments in your life in which something has deeply affected you."

Delilah, and I with her, sit for a long time staring at her blank page.

"Let's try the adjective game," I might say.

"What's an adjective again?" Delilah counters.

Delilah can't think of an adjective and no one of the hundreds of adjectives in my list seems to apply to her at this moment.

"How about I interview you?" Delilah shakes her head, looking down.

What's a student, or writing coach, to do?

Suddenly, Delilah pipes up. "The moment I was adopted," she says. "That was an important moment, but I don't remember what it was like before I came to America," she says, again dejected. "I was too young."

Delilah had been adopted from China when she was ten months old. Her mom had described to her the conditions of the orphanage in which she had spent her first months.

"My mom told me I was dropped off at a police station hours after I was born, but how am I supposed to write about that?"

After several weeks of writing the same story she was told over and over in different ways, we both agreed the essay was going nowhere.

"Let's put this essay aside," I said. "Let's try something else."

But Delilah was blocked. And more than that, she was discouraged. Nothing seemed to interest her. She couldn't find a way to begin or even think about beginning something new, for, it seems, the essay about her adoption was the one that was calling to be written, though she had no idea how to write it.

Finally, in a moment of exasperation (and inspiration, as it turns out), I turned to her and asked, "Do you ever remember your dreams? Or do you have a recurrent dream—a dream you dream again and again?"

"Yes," she said. "I think so."

"Do you have one you remember now?"

"Yes," she said.

"Could you write it?"

Here, with her permission, is what Delilah wrote:

> *I remember it being daytime. I was walking with two friends and the sky was blue. There were kids playing; all the stores were opening and bustling. Then suddenly everything changed; the skies grew dark and grey. All the stores were closed and had huge bars on the windows and doors. I remember seeing random bunches of trouble-making teenagers. Then I had the strong urge to get away from all the dangerous people, so I climbed up a fire escape and just sat at the top of the building watching all the crime and poverty happen. I remember feeling very anxious and uneasy. Then I climbed down to find a friendly face to borrow his or her phone to call for help. I found a store owner who was just closing up shop. He seemed both friendly and dangerous. I called my mom and English teacher. Neither answered. I assume they were asleep. Then I thought of a bunch of other people who could help, but I didn't call them because I knew they would either be sleeping or wouldn't want to drive all the way to my location. I was feeling very alone and abandoned. I felt like it was just me against all the hurt and corruption in the world.*

"Wow!" I said. "Has this ever happened to you in real life?"

"No," she said.

"Would your mom ever leave you in a place like this all by yourself?"

"No."

"Have you ever felt this way before—completely abandoned, in a dark place, behind bars?"

"Maybe before I was adopted?" she said, looking off into the distance.

Painful as the preverbal memory was, Delilah suddenly got excited about what she was writing—and actually smiled for the first time in the month or so we had been working together. In fact, until that time, I'm not sure I had ever seen her smile.

This was a breakthrough moment—for me and for her. Never before in my career helping students write college essays had I asked a student to recount a dream as a way into the writing (though I had done this as a matter of course when I was teaching Creative Writing.)

The next week, the same thing happened with another student—she was blocked—but this time, her English teacher had presented the class with a poem and asked each student to write a poem that began with a reflection on his or her name. Suddenly the floodgates opened and the student was able to write. She had not predicted that this "riff" on her name would be the seeds of her common app essay. She got in early decision to Oberlin, just by the way.

> *My name says little about me, yet somehow it comprises my entire identity.*
> *Both my parents are lawyers, which is unusual.*
> *And they both love their work, which is even more unusual.*
> *Growing up, being the precocious, defiant child I was, I vowed never to become a lawyer. I wanted to be an Egyptologist, then an actor, then a psychologist.*
> *None of these passions stuck as I shifted out of childhood and reached my teen years.*
> *Now, although my past self may be shaking her head in disbelief, I want to become a lawyer.*
> *Not a public defender like my dad or one of those lawyers who works on the computer and doesn't seem to have a title like my mom, no.*
> *Because of my personality where idealism and logic are somehow married, I want to be a social justice lawyer.*
> *What exactly does this type of lawyer do?*
> *In my head, I wear a shiny superhero outfit with the word "advocate" plastered across the front of my chest.*
> *I fly around Berkeley swooping in to stop old men from shouting lewd comments at uncomfortable-looking young girls.*
> *Then, I crawl down the halls of Berkeley High, listening for the murmur of a gay slur and informing people about the detrimental effects of those offensive words.*

I proceed to offer protection to the teenagers about to engage in unprotected sex, and then I educate them about the importance of contraception use (much to their chagrin).

Of course, then my realistic side kicks in.

It's easy to speak in hypotheticals when the future seems distant.

My career is a hazy storm cloud, visible and inevitable, but not quite close enough that I have to search my closet for a rain jacket and umbrella.

I know that one day I will have a stable job, one that most likely pales in comparison to my colorful fantasies.

But, in the mean time, why shouldn't I aim high?

We raise our children to believe that obstacles are always surpass-able.

We raise our children to believe that they can accomplish anything they set their minds to.

But, somehow, despite the previous idealism, fantasy stops and transforms, almost instantaneously, into cold, hard reality.

Teenagers are left lost, forced to dive head first into the black-and-white world they previously viewed as vivid and full of opportunity.

Leaves are no longer emerald, the sun glows a dim, sorrowful yellow, and creativity and idealism are no longer praised.

Yet, somehow, youth is depicted as the highlight of our lives.

And that terrifies me.

Inspiration can come from anywhere. But you must be willing to go anywhere to look for it—even into the dark and mysterious worlds of poetry and dreams. You never know what you will find.

Recently, on the hip and cool college info website *The Prospect,* I read a statement by a student writing her college essay that reflects what many students think and feel about the process:

My first draft was so incredibly formal that it made me want to puke. After I wrote my first draft, I sent it to 3 people and asked them to basically shred it to pieces. I basically came up with 10 drafts in 7 days but I took about a 5 day break so my mind could be fresh when I did my final draft. If I were to compare my final with my first, the changes are so so so dramatic and different.

When it comes to writing college essays—probably the most important essay you will ever write in your life—you may tend to freeze. You may have preconceptions about what you think a college essay should be, as we've discussed. In an effort to sound sophisticated and intelligent, you may be tempted to abandon your own natural style of writing in favor of a style that you think (wrongly) will make you look good. As a result, your essays can tend to be stilted and stiff.

Sometimes, however, if nerves get the better of you, it's a good idea to shake things up and open yourself to other possibilities. You can read other great college essays as a way to jumpstart your imagination and see what is possible.

Sometimes inspiration can be found in the most unlikely places, however—poetry, dreams or snippets of prose used at random. Let me give you another example.

As an exercise in loosening the soil and finding some yet-undiscovered seeds to throw into it, I sometimes have students write Found Poetry. This exercise is almost always successful. I would not say I invented it myself. I have the Dadaists to thank for that. But I have my own way of directing students to do it. Usually, I have five or six books at the ready. I like to choose books with very rich language, each in a different register. Often, for example, I use the Bible, a book of poetry by say, Jorie Graham or Walt Whitman, a book about science—quantum mechanics, for instance—and anything else that might provide inspiration.

For our purposes, I will use *The Slight Edge* by Jeff Olson, *An Episode in the Life of a Landscape Painter* by Cesar Aira and *The Five Things We Cannot Change*, by David Richo, because that's all I brought with me to Ojai, California, where I do most of my writing. Ah, I see I also have *Radical Judaism*, a gorgeously written book by Rabbi Arthur Green.

My directions: Pick up a book at random. Scan a page and locate a phrase, also randomly; then write it down. Keep going. You may add transitions naturally if they occur to you. Break the lines wherever you like. Here goes:

The air had turned a lead-grey color
We throw a lot of that, a generation's dose
To exhaust the painter's energy
A deeper truth
Than that of history
It was not the first time
The twitching would begin with
A slight quiver
It is always the moment of decision
They grant us their fearlessness
Planets permanently hidden
Thunderclap on thunderclap
This is the painting.

In this particular case, I did not add any of my own writing. I simply pulled phrases from the books I named.

Now what do you do with this little poem?

You could title it and leave it at that!

How about, *What I See When I Close My Eyes*

Or

A Life on the Verge of Art

The possibilities are endless.

Would you make this little poem your college essay? You could. Especially if the title said a lot about the poem's meaning to you and answered the question of the prompt.

Unlikely, however.

So what do you do with it?

You can view each little phrase as a seed. Sprinkle some water on the poem and see which seeds grow and which will not. And then begin free writing on whatever strikes your fancy.

I will demonstrate:

When I think about the moment, I see it as a painting. But how do you paint a feeling, a smell, the way the wind moves through the trees? So powerful was the experience that I found myself returning to the same spot, the same valley, the same swatch of waving grasses under the same scrub oak, year after year after year.

But neither the trees nor the grasses nor the self I brought to see them, had remained the same . . .

There, in the orange groves, walking silently, hands behind his back, was Krishnamurti himself. I was sixteen. He was well into his eighties. A few years later, in a dream, I saw him pass out of the customary white robes he wore in the orange groves and evaporate like steam into the warm and clear Ojai air . . .

My mother had thought to leave my father. "I'm going to California," she said. "And you're going with me."

This was my first visit to Ojai.

Then I could go on to describe what a turning point in my life this experience was. And it was. Here I am forty years later, writing this book from my perch above the scrub oak I just described!

When I wrote the found poem above as an illustration, I had no idea I would end up writing about my first exposure to Ojai. My mother went back to my dad, by the way. I was greatly relieved she didn't leave him. And over and over, I went back to Ojai.

Once again, the wand has found the wizard.

As I said, I have never seen this exercise fail. And what it shows is that there are no accidents. Our deepest wishes, lies and dreams, like molten lava buried deep below the surface of the earth, are looking for some way out.

And now the moment we've all been waiting for.

4: The Free Write™

> I write because I don't know what I think until I read what I say.
>
> —Flannery O'Connor

You have waited a long time for the most important step in the whole process—The Free Write.

So What Is Free Writing, Anyway?

> **It is writing absolutely everything that comes to mind on a *specific topic* without editing. Free Writing is a focused stream-of-consciousness in which you leave your inner critic/editor at the door.**

> **In contrast to my earlier directions for listing significant moments, in which I asked for bullet points and bullet points only, the *only* requirement of The Free Write is that you use full sentences.**

There are two reasons for this:

Bullet points sometimes give you the illusion you have something to say and then when you really try to say it, the idea goes *poof,* up in smoke. Perhaps you've had this experience.

Secondly, and this is what's so amazing, if you really get *into* your Free Write, you will be able to use from 70 to 90 percent of what you've written.

In fact, as you get better and better at Free Writing, you will be able to use more and more of the material you Free Write.

When I ask students to Free Write on a given topic, which usually means a "moment" they've identified either in the process of listing significant moments in their lives (Plan A), the Five-Adjective Game (Plan B) or in The Interview (Plan C), I say:

Write everything that comes to mind about this moment/experience.

Write for ten minutes without stopping. You can, of course, keep going if you're on a roll. (It helps calm students if they think they will only be writing for a short time).

Like a magician with a hat full of colored scarves all knotted together, pull one color at a time, the pink scarves for example—pull, pull, pull— until there are no more pink scarves tied to each other left. Then pull the blue. The yellow. And so on. If, when you are pulling the blue, it teases up the yellow, open another document and write a sentence that will help you remember this idea, so you can go back to it later or bracket it, as I have done below.

Here is a Free Write about the day I met the prime minister of Israel, which doesn't begin with meeting him:

> I was living on Potrero Hill in San Francisco and had no idea just a year later I would take a post teaching in Israel. Rabin's wife had told him to put on his bulletproof vest the day he was shot. He was going to a peace rally—why did he need a bulletproof vest? So he had refused. He was so confident that he would be fine that he said he didn't need it. I watched it on television. The television was on this old dresser that was there when I got there. I had just moved to this house because the house I was living in had burned down. My partner had put boxes on the heater...By the time we got home, the house had burned down... [Tell the story of the fire.] I arrived in Israel with the name of one person, a friend of a friend whose mother was in the

Knesset (Israeli Parliament) my two dogs, Huck and Ella, and a lot of excitement about living in the Holy Land…

Actually, if I went on to attempt to write the essay about actually meeting the prime minister of Israel, I might find it was a dead end. Maybe I have a few things to say about it, but somehow it just doesn't give me enough to go on. Who cares? That's OK.

But maybe the story of how the house burnt down and what that meant—maybe that's the story that wants to be told.

That's perfectly fine. My essay does not *have* to be about the time I met the Israeli prime minister, although that would certainly look good on my resume! It can very well be about the time I lost my house to fire. Who says that wouldn't be a good topic? It's not prestigious. In fact, it was devastating.

But it was transformative too. A new life for me rose out of the ashes.

So you see, it's almost a spiritual process if you do The Free Write this way.

You can find inspiration anywhere, and you never know where it is going to take you.

That's why you have to be free. Trying to fit yourself into a box will only lead to *that which shall not be named!*

Some people speak about the left brain and right brain. I have never been able to keep them straight. Which one does which?

What I do know is that the creative, juicy, alive, mysterious, generative, associative, deep, inspired part of the brain becomes tiny and mute in the presence of *the inner critic/judge/organizer.*

I had a friend when I was a kid who had two Japanese fighting fish. One night, during a sleepover party at her house, one of them devoured the other.

Before going to sleep, I remember staring at them for a long time, their fancy, elaborate blue fins like diaphanous curtains swaying this way and that in the clear, illuminated water of the fish tank.

When we woke up, strands of blue were floating in the murky water.

Apparently, Japanese fighting fish will devour each other if left to their own devices but will die of loneliness if made to live in total isolation.

To keep Japanese fighting fish, you must put up a glass barrier so that the fish can see each other, but not eat each other alive.

So it is with the creator and the critic within you.

If you let them near each other, the critic will *always* win. It will, in fact, devour that small, still voice within.

The creative voice, in most of us anyway, is like the smallest seedling in a field of snow.

**It must be cultivated and protected.
Don't let the inner critic near it.**

Here are what some well-known writers have had to say on the subject:

> What I did discover, however, when I sat down to write my first, full-length nonfiction work, was that a new inner critic materialized out of the shadows with her own set of no-nos. She blew on my heart instincts and her dry-ice breath often smothered my creative joy...

> —Gail Godwin, "A Novelist Breaches the Border to Non-Fiction"

> Writing is finally a series of permissions you give yourself to be expressive in certain ways. To invent. To leap. To fly. To fall. To find your own characteristic way of narrating and insisting without being too self-excoriating. Not stopping too often to reread. Allowing yourself, when you dare to think it's going well (or not too badly), simply to keep rowing along...

> —Susan Sontag, "Directions: Write, Read, Rewrite, Repeat Steps 2 and 3 as Needed"

A blank page is scary. Trying to fill it with perfection is even scarier. That is why it's good to get as much as you can out and down before you worry about what you're going to do with it.

Free Writing is a way to tame the beast.

After all, in a Free Write, there's no need for structure or organization; you don't need to know what you're talking about; you don't need to spell things correctly; you don't need to begin, progress and conclude.

All you need to do is write your heart out—*in full sentences.*

In an essay entitled "To See Your Story Clearly, Start by Pulling the Wool Over Your Own Eyes," the late Kent Haruf describes it like this:

> I remove my glasses, pull a stocking cap down over my eyes and type the first draft single-spaced…in the actual and metaphorical darkness behind my closed eyes, trying to avoid being distracted by syntax or diction or punctuation or grammar or spelling or word choice of anything else that would block the immediate delivery of the story. I write an entire scene or section on one side of one page, in a very concentrated and incomplete way. I'm trying to avoid allowing the analytical part of my mind into the process too soon. Instead, I'm trying to stay in touch with subliminal, subconscious impulses and to get the story down in some spontaneous way.

As I mentioned, you'll get good at this if you keep doing it.

But again, as I also said, when you do get good, don't get seduced into thinking you can skip this step.

Or let's put it this way, if you hit a roadblock, remember to *Free Write!*

In terms of your college essay, I highly recommend it. Not only does it free you—as the name of the exercise implies—but it promises much more depth and complexity and richness in the final product. *Why?* Because even *you* don't know where The Free Write will take you. It's a mystery yet to be discovered.

> In truly good writing no matter how many times you read it you do not know how it is done. That is because there is a mystery in all great writing and that mystery does not dissect out. It continues and it is always something valid. Each time you re-read you see or learn something new.

> —Ernest Hemingway, On Writing

Free Writing is easy.

And it's organic.

And it's free!!

This may all seem strange to you (or not).

Why would you want to write yourself into mystery when you want to end up in clarity?

Once I was snorkeling in Mexico. We went out on the open sea first. It was a gray and overcast day and the sea was choppy. In fact, I remember looking down at the fish beneath me and seeing the anchor of our little skiff dragging and bouncing on the coral in the opposite direction from our snorkeling party.

Soon our guide, Antonio, called us in.

There were three guys from Italy on our expedition. They had talked the entire hour we motored out to sea. My partner and I were amazed at how loud they were. Everything they said, they seemed to shout to one another.

What was really crazy is that they continued this *underwater!* Amidst the sound of the groupers chomping on the coral, we could hear the Italians, exclaiming into their snorkels, *Que bella! Que magnifico!*

The sea was too rough that day for good snorkeling. Our boat lost its anchor. And the choppiness was clouding up the water.

Antonio decided we would instead snorkel in the river, fresh water, through the mangroves.

Unfortunately, during the hour boat ride back, I started to feel queasy and spent most of the time stretched out on the bottom of the boat—as close to my center of gravity as possible—that is, when I wasn't throwing up over the side of it. I could have left that detail out—the part about vomiting—but I've left it in, not only because it's true—it was also true Antonio had dreadlocks—but like the river, when I write, I follow the currents that take me.

When we got to the mangrove river, we took off our fins and walked two miles up river, snorkeling gear in hand. It was a rough two miles. I'm from New York City. My feet were used to shoes.

Once we reached our destination, Antonio told us to jump in the river and *go with the flow.*

And so, one by one, we did just that.

The Italians, by the way, decided to stay behind. It was just my partner and me, Antonio our guide, and the mangrove river before us.

I felt like Superman!

When you drift in the current of a river this way, it's a good idea to put your arms out in front of you. There are branches and roots and things to watch out for.

It was amazing.

In contrast to the murky, cloudy salt water in the open sea, the river was perfectly clear. I felt like someone had Windexed my mask.

Mangroves, as you may know, have their roots in the river. So when you look down, you see fish swimming in and out of the roots.

But you cannot just look down.

You must watch where you're going.

The ideal position to be in while snorkeling in a mangrove river is with half your mask below the surface of the water, the other half above. That way you can see the spectacle below you and make sure you don't collide with whatever lies ahead.

I have always found the experience of snorkeling through the mangroves to be a perfect metaphor for where good writing comes from. Partly a conscious, thoughtful, knowledgeable place—and partly from "underwater," from some place below the surface of consciousness, a trance-like place, a place of mystery where fish swim in and out and between the roots.

I often say to students embarking on The Free Write: Don't think! And I kinda mean it.

The more you just write write write, the better it will be.

A time will come to *do* something with The Free Write, but not until you have pulled out every connected scarf of every different color, until you have utterly exhausted (at least for the moment) every possibility, until there is no more to write.

Once you have committed to a Free Write, by the way, you have a certain responsibility to the gods of writing.

Whenever you have an idea, you must seize the moment to write it down.

To go back to our garden metaphor: You have thrown your seeds to the wind. Now you must harvest them even if they're wayward and growing in the garden next door or decide they need your attention in the middle of the night.

I have often gotten out of bed—grudgingly, I have to admit—to write down a sentence that comes to me or to jot down an idea so I can tend to it later. The times I have not done this, the idea has gone poof like smoke in the wind.

The gods of the art will smile on you if you jot down your ideas when they come to you.

You will see. More ideas will come your way because they will feel that the environment you are creating is hospitable. After all, you have prepared the ground, planted the seeds, and watered. Anything that wants to grow may come to you. This means you may get more weeds among your perfect little purebreds. That's OK. You can edit them out later.

If you have gotten this far and have free written your heart out, you've come a long way and have broken the back of this process. Congratulate yourself. And go do something else. You'll need to be clear and fresh for what comes next.

The Four Modes of Writing:

Showing, Telling, Analyzing and Reflecting

What most students—and the people helping them—don't realize when they're writing their college essays is that all of these "modes" of writing come into play in the narrative personal statement. Students are used to writing five-paragraph analytical essays. In fact, this particular mode of writing—the five paragraph essay—has been so ingrained in students that it is difficult to get them to write in any other way.

In an effort to pry them off of the dock and get them in the water, their English teachers, college counselors and essay coaches quote the familiar, but misleading rule of thumb: Show Don't Tell. A more accurate rule of thumb, as we have said, might be Show and Tell, and, I would add, Reflect.

At the moment either right before I have students free write, or after they have done an initial Free Write, before I bring in the W's (Who, What, Where, When and How?) and have them expand their Free Write (explained on next page), I like to speak to them about the four modes of writing.

Chances are, if they have already done a Free Write, they have been telling and not showing. Here is an example:

"Last summer I had an amazing conversation with my cabin mate, Josh. He and I sat around the campfire for hours telling each other our deepest secrets."

"Bring it to life!" I often say to students. And they look at me as if I'm speaking a foreign language.

"What does that mean?" they ask.

"It means, take what you have described and show it!"

"How do you do that?" they ask.

And that's when I speak to them about the four modes of writing—and more specifically, about the elements involved in showing. No one ever tells them that!

I begin by writing the four modes of writing at the top of a piece of paper:

Telling   Showing   Analyzing   Reflecting

I point to the Free Write they have just handed me.

"What you have here is telling," I say. "Analyzing is what you usually do in your five-paragraph essays.

Showing involves one or more of the following: Action, Description and Dialogue.

And finally, reflecting is what you do when you think about what you've just described: What did this mean to me? How did I feel? Why is this important? What might this show about me or about the choices I might make in the future?"

Let me illustrate.

Take the sentence you just wrote:

Last summer I had an amazing conversation with my cabin mate, Josh. He and I sat around the campfire for hours telling each other our deepest secrets.

Now let's add dialogue.

"Wanna sit here?" Josh said.

Now description:

It was almost twilight. The sun was streaming through the redwoods. We could see a swarm of gnats having a party by the picnic table.

And now, action:

Before I could answer, Josh grabbed a chair, held my shoulders and pushed me down into it.

And some more dialogue: *"Okay," I said. "I guess I do wanna sit here!"*

Description, Action and Dialogue are all sub-categories of Showing.

As you can see from what I've written, adding dialogue, description and action *shows* what is going on without your having to say it—and in the process, creates a vivid, see-able, feel-able, taste-able, touch-able, hear-able scene that brings the moment to life by appealing to the five senses.

Once you have done this, it is natural to want to reflect upon it: *I had been wanting to talk to Josh all summer, but had been too shy to speak to him. Now sitting across from him beside the fire, I felt moved and warm and excited all at the same time.*

Reflection adds depth to the moment—it expresses how you feel, think, felt or thought about a specific experience.

Next time you do a Free Write, take a look at it and see whether you are really showing through dialogue, action and description, and reflecting, by adding your thoughts and feelings, or merely telling what happened. Be aware of the modes of writing you are using—and see whether there is a way to go back and bring the scene you have just written to life.

5. The Expanded Free Write

The beauty of having written a Free Write is that you no longer have a blank page—

you have spewed your guts out (perhaps there was indeed a reason I told you about the unfortunate state of my stomach in the chapter before).

There is far less risk of *that which shall not be named*— because you have something to work with!

I'd like now to play a little game, to do an experiment. Below you will find one paragraph of a Free Write.

What I'd like you to do is pick up a pen or pencil and write questions in the margins of The Free Write—stuff you want or need to know for it to make sense.

> Eight years later, Michael, a close friend of mine and fellow co-president of our high school's club told his family's story to the rest of the club, "My grandparents watched as their home was demolished. They were left with only the things they could carry on their backs." Michael spoke as he sat in the green and black chair, which is designated for the person who has come forth to share his or her story at each Dialogue Club meeting. The bell sounded, and I proceeded to Spanish class pondering his words. Every Tuesday morning, Michael and I make our way over to room 203 during our fifteen-minute morning break for club meetings.

Reading this Free Write you might ask:

What happened eight years earlier?
What kind of club is this?
When did this event occur? What grade were you in?
Why are you telling me this?

Here's another Free Write. This one is written by Olivia Sterling-Maisel.

> My desk is permanently engraved with the memory of Camp Tuolumne. The night my camp went up in flames was one of the

loneliest moments I have ever experienced. It felt like all the memories I have ever made there were gone forever. And I was afraid of forgetting. So I took a big green pen, the exact color of the pine trees that had filled the camp, and wrote all over my desk. I filled it with every memory I could think of, until it was nothing but a sea of meaningless words that when put together made up the happiest times of my life. And in the center I engraved the song that echoed in my thoughts every night that I was there, and every night since. This song was sung every day as the sun was setting against the gorgeous forest that surrounded camp.

After reading Olivia's Free Write, you might want to know:

What happened?
Why did the camp go up in flames?
Where is Camp Tuolumne?
What memories do you have of it?
What was the song that echoed in your thoughts?
What do you mean by "gorgeous forest?" Tell us what it looked like.
Were you there when it burnt down?
Did you have to evacuate?
Why was this camp so important to you?

This is much easier to do with someone else's writing than it is with your own. *You* experienced the experience and so all the details, backstory, context, dialogue are in your head. Often you *think* you've explained things clearly and fully, but, actually, you haven't done that at all.

This is why it's really useful to have a trusted reader look at your Free Write before you move on to the next step.

That's one of the main purposes of peer editing. Your reader can provide feedback on whether or not you've made something clear.

Not everyone is a good reader for you, by the way.

> **You have to make sure you really trust your reader—and that your reader "gets" you or "gets" what you're trying to do.**

But once you find that person, he or she is invaluable to you. It could be your English teacher; it could be your college counselor; it could be your best friend; it could be your mom or dad or sister or brother.

What you really need is someone who is going to tell you where you've left things out and ask you the questions that will help you write what I call an Expanded Free Write.

> **Once you've written your Free Write, you can call in the W's.**

- Where were you?

- When was this?

- Who were you with?

- What were you doing?

- How did you feel?

- What was important to you about that moment?

- Why do you think you remember it?

Recently, I have happened upon a great new way to help students expand their Free Writes. I was working with a student from Stockholm on Skype. In the Skype chat box, she sent me two paragraphs of her Free Write. I found myself highlighting sentences and asking questions that would help her expand on what she had written.

For example, she wrote:

My dad had decided he would teach me how to fly, so we set out for the tiny airport outside our village where my grandfather kept his little plane. There were all these dials and controls. The feeling was amazing.

I wrote:

How old were you? Can you remember the moment your dad asked you if you wanted to learn to fly? Can you remember moments watching your dad or grandfather fly a plane? Were you ever in the plane with them? Where was this air field? What did it look like? What was the dialogue between you and your dad? What did he say? What did you say? (You can reconstruct or approximate what you think was said). How did you get up into the plane? What did the plane look like? Roughly, how big was it? Did you pilot or co-pilot it? What did you see? Describe the feeling in your body. "Amazing" is abstract. Did you feel your stomach contract? What did you think about?

As you can see from this extensive list of questions, the moment the student chose to describe is very rich, but needs quite a bit of expansion so that the reader can see and feel what the writer is describing.

Sometimes, even with a student who is sitting across from me in my office, we go to Google Hangouts or some other online chatting space and go back and forth in writing without even speaking.

I have found this to be a new, and very effective, way to get students to expand what they have written.

Sometimes when I ask a question, the student will start to answer me orally.

"Write it down," I say.

And we go back to instant messaging each other until the Free Write is fully fleshed out.

Then what do you do after you expand The Free Write?

You go back to the drawing board, in a way, but this time, you're equipped.

You focus specifically on what needs to be filled in, and you Free Write again on whatever that is. As the title of Susan Sontag's essay on writing suggests: "Directions: Write, Read, Rewrite, Repeat Steps 2 and 3 as Needed."

The Expanded Free Write may be longer than The Free Write itself.

This will depend on how much you were able to plumb the depths of your soul the first time around.

But remember, you're still on *free* land. No fees. No grammar police. You don't even need paragraphs. Still just Free Writing!

6. How to Make Order Out of Chaos

Every block of stone has a statue inside it and it is the task of the sculptor to find it.

—Michelangelo

Beyond the chaos of The Free Write, there lies an order waiting to be discovered.

Were it not so, The Free Write would not write itself so freely. Order is there, somewhere. The question is how do you find it?

The first thing I usually do is choose a great opening sentence out of the pile of (seeming) junk.

(Specific examples of identifying an opening sentence follow a bit later.)

Just as when, in a house that has been empty for months, you must run the water a while before it clears, often the beginning of The Free Write is what I call "rusty water."

It's necessary, but not necessarily where the gems will be found.

Once you have located a possible first sentence, you have a starting point.

Like a holographic image, the starting point often has within it the whole trajectory of the essay or various possible routes.

Here are few sample openings. This first one is by Amos Goldbaum. It was the essay he sent to Pitzer to accompany his portfolio:

> When I draw I like to forget I'm drawing and then look into the face of a man I've never seen. The man has a nose like half an equilateral, and eyes with ambiguous and vestigial layers of skin. The upper lip might hang over his lower or maybe his mouth is open. The chin forms a nice arc, coming down and under his jawline and then splits into a dangling lobe of an ear. The brow is thick—caveman style—and the hair is scruffy. People ask, "Who is that?" My answer is as mysterious as the drawing itself. "I don't know." Every man is different, although my technique never varies. Most are profiles, in brutal staring contests with my left hand. The cheekbone is a slithering x-cubed line...

Usually, once I pinpoint a starting sentence, I can pretty quickly map a route.

Note:

Often the best sentence to start with is one that will land the reader right in the middle of the action.

Then you can explain what the context or backstory is later. This is what writing teachers are talking about when they say start in the middle. They mean, throw the reader into the deep end of the pool and make him or her swim!

Starting in the middle, for me, also means *not* starting with an introduction when you begin to work on your essay. Start anywhere *but* the introduction in the process of writing the essay.

From the Free Write above, I might pick out the line: People ask, "Who is that?" My answer is as mysterious as the drawing itself.

Or The brow is thick--caveman style--and the hair is scruffy.

Both of these openings start in the middle, not in the reflection, and create suspense.

On the subject of trying to write an introduction before you know what you want to say, I like to tell the following story because it perfectly illustrates the benefits of waiting to write the introduction:

I was on my way to back-to-school night. There was a full moon, I remember, yellow, hanging low over the horizon. I would have liked to take a picture. In fact, today, I'm sure I would have pulled my car over and done so. But this was the early days of cell phones—they did not yet have cameras. In fact, it may have been my very first cell phone that rang in the seat next to me. "Emergency appendectomy," Josie Johnson, the head of our department said. "Can you take over?"

The first group of five hundred eager parents filed into the auditorium. I was not new to speaking before large audiences. A few days before, I had given a lecture at Reed College to a substantial group, and earlier that year, I had been asked to read at The New York Public Library.

In this particular case, however, I was completely unprepared. Granted, I had been teaching for about fifteen years. But how would I describe what it is we do in the English department?

 For a long moment, I was silent. The audience waited. I waited. Finally, something burst out of my mouth!

"We read," I said. "That's right! We read works in many different genres. There's poetry, of course...Oh yes, and essays. We read essays. And novels. We also read novels..." Another long pause. "We write too! I mean, that's a very important part of our curriculum, writing is..." And so on and so on, until the next group of five hundred parents filed into the auditorium to hear the exact same speech.

The second time 'round, however, it was different.

This time, I began: "There are five basic areas we cover in the English department: reading, writing, grammar, vocabulary, and speech!" I spoke easily—and what I said was organized. I even **introduced** the subjects I would speak about!!

I never know what I think until I hear what I say. And I never know what I want until I see what I do. That was how I decided to become a writer instead of a doctor. That, in fact, is how I make most of the big decisions in my life. I look at what I do in order to know what I want.
In our world, sadly, teachers teach students to write essays from beginning to end. What a recipe for disaster. And high anxiety.

If you can locate a great opening sentence, you have come a long way!

The next step is to see whether it will provide you with a sense of what follows.

> From my opening sentence here I would speak about…then…and then go to…and end with…

What I have done here is as close as I ever get to a *rough outline*. And as you can see, when I say rough, I really mean rough. You don't even need numbers.

You can simply list keywords or phrases—in whatever order you decide—that will jog your memory so you know where to go when.

The next step involves excavation—a kind of search and rescue. This is what I call Lift and Drop.

It is predicated on your having written both a very exhaustive Free Write and Expanded Free Write. Without these, you are not going to have enough fuel for the fire, as it were.

You know where you're starting. You have made a rough outline of where you go from there. Now you go to your

> **draft and lift out sections that fill the requirements, roughly, of your rough outline. Once you have excavated the site, the first thing you'll most likely need is connective tissue.**

You've lifted sections and dropped them into place. Now, as if you were making a quilt, you're going to need to stitch them together.

There are no hard and fast rules for transitioning from one section or segment to another, but there are a few strategies for tying things together.

1. Start with dialogue, action, or a moment. *En medias res.* Or in cinematic terms: *a cold open.* Tell or fill out the story—rather than adding context or reflection—as if you're sitting around the campfire.

2. If necessary, provide a sentence or two of context (less is more here) so the reader will know what is going on.

3. Reflect on your story. What did you think, feel, imagine when this was happening? Or what do you think about it now?

4. Provide another anecdote or continue the original story.

5. Conclude with something that reflects on what you learned or how you changed or what you saw and how this might relate to the future (since that's what the Ad Com is wondering about), and, as with your opening sentence—end with a bang (not a whimper).

Here is a real life example, which I have annotated to demonstrate the process I have just described:

And then I blacked out. [Drops you into the moment. Creates suspense. What happened? Why?] In all honesty, I never really saw the guy who hit me, but soon after, I was staring at the sky. [Gives background to initial action] I had been set up for the worst hospital pass I have ever received in my career as a lacrosse player. [A bit of context] Up and over my head the ball went, and then up and over my head my feet went, into the air. [Back to a description of what happened, elaborating on previous action] As much as I would like to say I popped up immediately as if nothing happened, it wouldn't be true. I kept playing, clearly hazy, until my coaches prompted me to get off the field. [Answers question, what happened next?] Like many obstacles in my life, I never saw it coming. [Reflection on how this event relates to others in his life.]

Below is a student's Free Write, verbatim. I have highlighted sentences I thought would serve as good openings for the essay.

Jessica lonely and homeless and never crying. The past is a foreign country I don't have the paperwork to travel to. It was sometime in the afternoon on a weekday. Probably.

In young adult literature, our protagonist always remembers dates like these perfectly, but I am neither fictional nor in possession of an eidetic memory, so it could have been a Tuesday or a Friday or a leap year when I checked my phone and found her hours-old text. Six texts, in fact, the first five overflowing their 140-character limit. I can't remember what I said to my mom, or whether or not I was crying, although she swears I was and I swear I wasn't, but we left with the oven on and the side door unlocked and water for tea still in the microwave.

We circled her apartment for ten minutes before we realized that she had already left.

Her phone went straight to voicemail. Tracking down a teenage girl with a powered-off phone proved difficult. The fact that she was on foot was only marginally helpful. Eventually she called, using a cashier's personal cellphone, to give us directions so we could pick her up.

We found her, lower lip bleeding, but dry-eyed on the curb outside Taco Bell. She had her track and field bag, her phone (but not her charger), a newfound resolution, and a Burrito Supreme.

She looked monumentally calm for a fourteen-year-old who had just walked out on her family for the first time.

She climbed into the car quietly. I vaguely recall her assuring my mother that she would only need a few days and my mother assuring her that it was no trouble at all.

These are the facts, newly acknowledged that day, that remain seared indelibly in my memory: her father, the man who offered me rides home from school and cracked bad jokes in the front seat, had lost his job. Her father, the man who had promised her a new pair of running shoes for Christmas, had gambled away his severance pay. Her father, the only able-bodied parent she had, planned to do the same with their welfare. We had an empty apartment above the garage; she needed a place to stay.

My best friend became my housemate for two months, give or take.

Her parents threatened to split. "It wasn't so bad," I explained, "having divorced parents," as we ruined all my pillowcases with mascara-streaked tears. "Anyway, maybe they'll work it out," I comforted, "mine managed to, eventually." I did not mention that it took several heart palpitations and a minor stroke for them to do so. She already knew.

The three highlighted sentences or group of sentences I have chosen here seem like possible beginnings.

I would probably choose the second highlighted sentence, "We found her, lower lip bleeding, but dry-eyed," because it creates suspense, it locates a moment in time and space, it's vivid and picture-able—and because it's powerful. From there, you can always go on to provide context or backstory so the reader knows the relevant event that led to this moment.

Usually—and this is the beauty of it—you can literally *Lift and Drop* pieces of The Free Write into a new document to get a working rough draft.

Note: There are infinite possibilities. The person doing the choosing is doing so from his or her own unique (and often, unconscious) perspective. How you work with a Free Write—what you choose to include and what you choose to exclude—this is what makes your essay different from mine.

Here is a sample essay I might put together from this student's Free Write. Yours (and hers, as it turned out) will be different from the one I have constructed:

> We found her, lower lip bleeding, but dry-eyed on the curb outside Taco Bell. She had her track and field bag, her phone (but not her charger), a newfound resolution, and a Burrito Supreme. She looked monumentally calm for a fourteen-year-old who had just walked out on her family for the first time.
>
> I can't remember what I said to my mom, or whether or not I was crying, although she swears I was and I swear I wasn't, but when we left to look for Jessica, we left the oven on and the side door unlocked and water for tea still in the microwave.
>
> We circled her apartment for ten minutes before we realized that she had already left. Her phone went straight to voicemail. Tracking down a teenage girl with a powered-off phone proved difficult. The fact that she was on foot was only marginally helpful. Eventually she called, using a cashier's personal cellphone, to give us directions so we could pick her up.
>
> She climbed into the car quietly. I vaguely recall her assuring my mother that she would only need a few days and my mother assuring her that it was no trouble at all.
>
> Her parents threatened to split. I tried to reassure her. "It wasn't so bad," I explained, "having divorced parents," as we ruined all my pillowcases with mascara-streaked tears. "Anyway, maybe they'll work it out," I comforted, "mine managed to, eventually." I did not mention that it took several heart palpitations and a minor stroke for them to do so.
>
> She already knew.
>
> These are the facts, newly acknowledged that day, that remain seared indelibly in my memory: her father, the man who offered me rides home from school and cracked bad jokes in the front seat, had lost his job. Her father, the man who had promised her a new pair of running shoes for Christmas, had gambled away his severance pay. Her father, the only able-bodied parent she had, planned to do the same with their welfare. We had an empty apartment above the garage; she needed a place to stay.

In young adult literature, our protagonist always remembers dates like these perfectly, but I am neither fictional nor in possession of an eidetic memory, so it could have been a Tuesday or a Friday or a leap year when I checked my phone and found her hours-old text. Whatever day it was, I saw through the rabbit hole of childhood from the other side and caught a glimpse of the adult world into which I would soon be heading.

Again, this is only one of infinite possibilities. I don't think it's necessarily "the best," but I just want to give you an idea of how a draft can be put together from a Free Write.

> **Once you have a working rough draft—
> something with a beginning, a middle and at
> least a hint of an end—you are ready to revise.**

7. Techno-Logy

Observing myself closely helping students write their essays—in real time, in actual sessions with actual students—I realized that I had been using certain aspects of technology, as I just mentioned—at various stages in the process—to great effect.

The more global and far-reaching my clientele has become, the more I have had to rely on Skype to communicate with students in Hong-Kong, London, Sydney—all over the world. As a result, I have stumbled upon certain methods, aided by technology, that actually are very useful.

In the course of these Skype sessions, particularly as I am asking a student to describe to me one of his or her significant moments—or once I have read a Free Write and am wanting to know more—I ask the student to IM me on Skype chat. In fact, I sometimes even ask students not to speak, but rather to write whatever thoughts they are having at the moment instead. And I have even been known to ask a student sitting right in front of me if we could Instant Message each other instead of talk!

Here is a great example of a Skype chat I had with a student:

Lizzy: I would dream about the robot and I would go to sleep wondering what the next solution to the problem would be and then I would wake up knowing the answer.

Gabrielle Glancy: Specifically, what solution were you looking for and what was the dream that brought you to it?

Describe the dream in detail.

What did the robot look like?

Did it have a name?

Did it have a personality?

Lizzy: The robot was not gray metal like you would think. It had a warm and soft belly and red sleeves and was called "Tommy." And these deep brown eyes you could look into. It didn't really look back at you, but when you looked into its eyes, it was like you could see worlds in it...

Long Pause.

Gabrielle Glancy:

Why were you building a robot?

What were your goals in doing so?

What was the process like?

For a project at school? On your own?

What were the obstacles?

Lizzy: It was for a program called FIRST Tech Challenge, where the robot would have a task based on a sports model that changed from year to year.

So this year was a combination of soccer and basketball... And the robots fit in a cubic foot.

Gabrielle Glancy: Specifically? For example, we were tasked with creating a robot that could both throw a basketball into the hoop and kick a soccer ball into the goal... I don't know anything about this stuff. I'm just making it up. We were given the following parameters...

Lizzy: Okay. I get it. We were tasked with creating a robot that could take whiffle balls and golf balls and put them into cylindrical goals of varying heights. And then push them into marked goals on the playing field. The competition was comprised of three parts. The first was a thirty-second autonomous period in which the robot had to rely on sensors to navigate the field and release the balls onto the field by knocking over a kickstand. Before the round begins, you are assigned to a random team as your partner to play against another team of two. There was a two minute "teleop" period in which the robot was controlled by a human player to collect the most balls in the goals. The robot had a size constraint and couldn't reach the goals without some sort of lift mechanism. We started out with a rack-and-pinion lift, but the weight of the lift would cause the pieces to fall out. So I was wondering how to structurally support the beams. And then I dreamed that the pieces could fit within the robot if we cut the channels out.

Lizzy: It taught me project management

Lizzy: We would stay up until 2 a.m. listening to whatever music there was on the radio

Gabrielle Glancy:

What did the robot look like?

Did you name it?

Lizzy: We knew that there were only five hours left before we had to go to competition and it wasn't done yet.

Gabrielle Glancy: What skills did you need to possess to build it? How does this project relate to your intellectual goals, if at all? Are you interested in AI?

Lizzy: It was quiet aside from the music and occasional sounds of wrenches clattering on the ground

We all knew that we had a role to fill

We would notice things about each other

Lizzy: When someone was struggling with a nut, someone else would help hold the flat wrench while another would screw it in with an Allen wrench.

Lizzy: It was a perfect synergy in which nothing needed to be said.

Lizzy: We were working as a unit instead of as a group of individuals.

Lizzy: Despite being exhausted from lack of sleep, I was feeling energetic.

And here is Lizzy's essay on the subject:

My first Lego robot, shiny and smooth with plastic bits held together by black pegs, was controlled by a brick that looks kind of like Karel, Stanford's virtual robot used in CS106a. It had a light sensor and could follow a black line on a white table, to see it move like a snake, back and forth across the table like it was alive. IBM's Watson, the supercomputer that won Jeopardy, quickly became my new fascination. The developers of Watson gained much of my empathy and adulation after I watched a documentary on the process used to build it. I learned of its initial failures.

A year later, my team made it to regionals. Everything seemed artificially colored, like a dream almost. Except in a dream I wouldn't have my friend screaming at me for mis-calibrating the light, and losing us a match. She slapped me. It didn't hurt physically, but tears started running down my cheeks. I resolved to never yell at a teammate like she yelled at me that day. An incognito judge saw the display and marked us down for teamwork. Our robot's detachable parts and the wheel that made it perfectly equidistant from the wall were deemed too advanced for a rookie team, so the judges concluded that the robot must have been built by one of our parents. The robot that made it so far was now stuttering from a myriad of problems. We sat there on the bleachers expectantly, hoping to make it to States. But our team was never called up.

On the drive home, I had this empty feeling pressing on my chest. The adrenaline rush was gone. I worked hard but it wasn't enough.

Ever since I was little, I had a fondness for programming. The computer was the one thing in the world that would do exactly what I told it to— in the most infuriating way possible. There's a joke, a programmer's wife tells him, "Go to the store and buy a loaf of bread, and if they have eggs, get a dozen." The programmer comes home with twelve loaves of bread. As an aside, I've come to realize that programmer culture from the inside has a heavy emphasis on masculinity... Women are looked down upon if they're too feminine. The hypocrisy lies in the fact that programming was invented by a woman named Ada Lovelace. The ingrained image of a "programmer" from outsiders or dilettantes is that of a guy with no friends who never sees the light of day and sits in his dark cramped cave lit only by the eerie blue glow of his multiple monitors.

You could see Watson's thought process in the electron-like cloud of teal-blue wisps that flew around his face like a swarm of bees. Maybe if Watson could look back at me out of his penetrating, visionless eyes, this is how I might appear to him. He might think, if indeed he is capable of thought, that he is looking in the mirror.

This is a beautiful Free Write, as you can see, and much of it made it into the final draft.

Reflecting on process, I want to mention two other techniques I have adopted as a direct result of working with students remotely.

Labeling/Clumping Sections

One technique I have found very useful is to ask students to go back to their Free Writes, or better yet, their Expanded Free Writes—and label their clumps. If the Free Write came out as a butterfly, or has evolved from larvae to caterpillar and has a discreet, albeit, furry form, this technique won't be necessary.

But for those Free Writes that are amorphous, truly stream-of-consciousness, it is sometimes useful to label each section in broad strokes in order to be able to move sections around.

In one particularly memorable case, these named sections were so funny and ironic, and created such interesting counterpoint or juxtaposition with their original sections, that we decided to keep the labels in the final draft.

Sharing the screen

Finally, especially when the rough or first draft needs to be shaken up or line and copy editing needs to be done, I have found it really useful to put the document into WORD, track changes, and share the screen with the student. This can happen in the reverse as well. You can ask the student to share the screen with you and you can literally watch her as she goes through the draft making changes. You can then either comment in words, "What made you take that section out?" Or, you can resort to Skype chat once again to allow the student to respond in writing to whatever clarification or expansion needs to be done. Google docs is another option, of course. For my purposes, however, I find it easier to keep track of previous drafts—and to keep them pristine—using WORD.

This makes the process of editing and line-editing *live*.

When I do this, I also notice that I pause and comment on the meta-level about what I am suggesting the student do. I might, for example, say, "Let's shake this up and put the last paragraph first!"

The student gasps.

"Let's just play with it and see what it does to your essay."

"So you see," I might say, "There are not a million ways to write an essay—there are infinite ways!"

And it is true.

I want the student to unfix herself from the original order in which her ideas came out. Chronological order is indeed very addictive and enslaving. It's often how a story comes out at first if a student is anxious and cannot really, honestly follow the random flow of her thoughts. And once a story is written in chronological order, it seems nearly impossible to get students to shake it up. Sometimes, when I even suggest it, they look at me as if I'm suggesting blasphemy.

This is when sharing the screen—and getting feedback from someone who is not emotionally attached to the ideas—can be invaluable. I just pop a random (though very vivid) moment at the top and say, "So where would you go from here?"

"You use instant messaging to help students write their essays?" an appalled English teacher said to me one day over his readers. He must have been having a particularly Luddite moment.

I must admit to having had some embarrassment myself when I first realized that to be true to my process and the elements in it that have contributed to my success, I just had to include this chapter—as if the use of technology were somehow cold, or gimmicky, sophomoric or shallow. But I have gotten over that now.

I am confident that as I continue to work with students remotely, I will continue to export whatever techniques I have found useful on Skype to my in-person sessions.

After all, words themselves, are a form of technology—tools we use to communicate the ineffable cloud of teal-blue wisps that swarm inside our heads.

I have come to think of the current technological state we inhabit as evolutionary, organic to who we are as a species at this moment in time. Natural Selection. Survival of the fittest. If it works—it will prevail.

And, for better or worse, have come to think of myself, and of us all, as both progenitors and descendents of Watson, in the light of all his/her/their eerie blue glory.

8: RE-Vision

Think about the word itself. *Re-Vision*. It is about seeing with new eyes.

Again, you will need both time and feedback to do this.

All writers have trusted readers, editors, proofreaders—or all three—to help them out. It is not a sign of weakness to ask for help. Since we know who we are (somewhat, anyway), it is easy to think that we have communicated what is in our minds directly onto paper and that it should be perfectly clear to the reader. We need others to tell us whether and to what extent this is true.

The best test I know to see whether your essay is interesting is: Read it out loud.

Go into the bathroom where the acoustics are good and belt the thing out. If at any point your mind wanders, you want to rush through a particular passage, or, even worse, your eyes glaze over, you can bet the Ad Com is already asleep. Mark that section as one that must either be revised or taken out!

As in a poem, in your college admissions essay, which is only 500 to 650 words long, you must *make every word count.*

Next, the best test of whether what you have written is understood the way you want it to be by someone else is to get feedback.

Let your reader ask questions: What did you mean here? When did that happen? Why was that important to you? And you ask questions of your reader, too:

Did you understand the conclusion? Did the essay grab you right away? Was the part about my brother scary or just depressing?

Once you have a sense of what needs to be done, you've got to find creative ways to do it.

You may realize, for example, that the reader doesn't have enough information about a certain moment; the details are too vague; more context may be needed. You've got to fill in the picture if it is to make sense. Similarly, you may see that the order of ideas is not quite working as it is. You have to play with it until you get it just right.

I would not say this is always easy. In fact, almost always, there's at least a little bit of pain involved in writing, especially at the revision stage of the process. Writing is like giving birth. Something that has never existed has to be brought into the world.

You may have to break a sweat at times to get the order of ideas right or to sufficiently fill out the details. Don't panic. Just remember: You might feel pain; push through it to the other side.

Stay focused. Figure out what needs to be done and don't stop until you find a way to do it. (Unless you need the perspective a little distance can give you. In that case, take a break and come back to it.)

Don't be afraid of the pain.

Or of the chaos. It's all part of the process.

Recently, I read an article about the writer Anne Carson in *The New York Times* in which she describes the experience of writing her most recent book. The process, she says, "was a mess, obstacle course, uphill grapple in the dark, almost totally disoriented and discontented experiment every minute of the thousand or so years it took to work out."

That about says it. You must "grow accustomed to the dark." Work hard. And hold the hope that there will be light at the end of the tunnel.

Luckily, if you have written a Free Write, you will have put the pain off as long as possible in order to get your ideas out in a worry-free zone.

It is much easier to rearrange, cut, add detail, refine, expand, and enliven, than it is to pull a finished product out of thin air.

So there is pain. But there must also be play.

Take the spirit of The Free Write with you wherever you go.

Be willing to cut the whole thing up into pieces, sentence by sentence, put it in a paper bag, shake it up, and see where the sentences fall.

Be open to alternatives. Try things out. And again, get feedback where and when you need it.

When someone you really trust says, "I don't get this; this doesn't make sense to me; I don't understand," believe him or her.

It is sometimes difficult to let go of a phrase or passage you're particularly attached to.

In fact, when I was in college, I had a professor who devised an experiment to show how deeply and easily people get attached. He passed out potatoes to the class, asked us to speak to, admire, and caress our potatoes for the entire length of the lecture, and then had designated students in the class come around and collect our potatoes into large, black garbage bags. He then picked up a knife and cut them up into little pieces right in front of our eyes. People were weeping!

Human beings have a (huge) propensity to get (fairly deeply) attached to anything they care for (in a relatively short time)—even a potato!

Perhaps it is obvious why, in a book about writing, I have taken the time to tell this story.

The word on the page—if you have written it—is like your baby. This is normal human behavior. It's probably even healthy human behavior.

But attachment can be an obstacle to good writing.

Sometimes, one must take a butcher knife to what one has written. It is best if some time has passed between the writing and the editing, for this reason, among others, so that the sadness is a little less acute.

Above all, don't get too attached to your potato!

I call the time between the writing and the editing "marination."

It's a good idea. I highly recommend it. It's particularly good after you've written your first solid draft.

Sometimes, in my own writing, there are phrases I can't seem to part with, though the consensus may be that the work flows better without them. Sometimes I even know this at the time. Sometimes I see it later, even after publication.

Similarly, sometimes, even when I have given a student the space and distance needed to gain perspective, I have found myself editing out a phrase that is awkward, grammatically incorrect, and clearly (to me anyway) detracting from what the student is trying to get across, only to find it back again in the next draft sent to me. Sometimes this happens all the way to the bitter end.

The student just cannot part with that particular phrase, no matter how hard he or she tries, no matter how many times I make the case for its being cut—the student is simply attached to his potato!

Be willing to sacrifice your potato for a cabbage, a Brussels sprout, or even a strawberry if these work better and make the essay stronger.

You must not take constructive criticism personally, and you must not be too attached to what you have written. You must be willing to sacrifice the good for the great or the great for the good, if it leads to the greater good. ;-)

In other words, you must be a Buddha when you receive feedback.

Because virtually all college essays have a word limit, it is easy to be tempted, as you go through the process of revision, to start worrying about cutting your essay down to size. Don't do it.

You must remember that you are right in the middle of the process and must keep going before you do any cutting.

You must roll out the dough before you cut the cookies.

This is what I tell students when they are tempted to bring their machetes in before the process of expansion and revision has fully taken place.

When you have said all you can say, then it is time to do the cutting.

The floodgates opened; you found your voice. You were definitely on a roll. And now you have 2,367 words to fit into an essay that needs to be under 650. What are you going to do?

This is always a crucial moment in the writing process.

At this point when I am working in person with a student, I ask him or her to bring in two hard copies. We sit side by side, with an invisible barrier between us, and begin the hard work of trimming the fat. I would never take on this task of cutting someone else's essay myself. That would be akin to plagiarism—and I would just feel too bad about all the precious words that ended up on the cutting room floor. At the same time, if a student does it without me, the draft I get is missing what was cut out—obviously. Sometimes I find myself remembering a passage from six drafts ago and wanting it back. And sometimes I remember something is missing, but I cannot for the life of me reconstruct what it was.

So this side-by-side method seems to work really well. Then we compare notes. If we have both cut the same lines or sentences, we can be pretty sure, it's fine for them to go.

Sometimes, however, at the moment you are ready to cut, you may catch a glimpse of what is missing. In this case, you must go back to the drawing board, in a sense, and free write on that particular moment, description or idea.

"But now it's going to be even longer!" you might say.

And I would answer, as I always, do, "That's Okay. Again, you must roll out the dough before you cut the cookies."

So remember, don't start cutting until you are confident you have written everything you can write, until you have expanded, developed and fleshed out your essay. And be prepared for this process to happen more than once, or twice, or three times. You must do what it takes to produce the fullest, most expressive and fully realized essay possible.

9. What Kind of Language Makes Strong Writing Strong?

> Don't tell me the moon is shining; show me the glint of the light on the broken glass.
>
> —Anton Chekhov

What makes strong writing strong is that the reader can feel it, taste it, hear it, see it.

Images *bring* what is being described to life. Metaphors and similes make it vivid. Specific details make what you are writing palpable and memorable.

The Free Write is not really a time to add specifics, images, or detail—unless they flow naturally the first time round. It's a time to get it all out.

> **The Expanded Free Write is a good moment to slow down and pull out all the literary stops. You may also do this after you have written the rough or first draft.**
>
> **When you are describing a feeling, for example, you can try to locate it in your body or imagine what that feeling might feel like if you rubbed it against the palm of your hand.**

Let me give you an example.

You could say, after a fight with a good friend, at that terrible moment when you are uncertain whether repair will be possible or not:

I felt very sad.

Or you could say:

I could not get rid of this feeling inside me, much as I tried. It was like a lost boat drifting between my throat and my stomach in water that was dark even on the brightest day of the year.

> ## When you speak about someone or something, name them/it.

My sister gave me her snack.
Or, better: My sister, Hannah, gave me her pretzels.

> ## Create pictures for the reader.

Her hair was the color of painted gold.
She had such a large gap between her two front teeth, her tongue kept popping out between it when she spoke.

Poetry does what I am describing as a matter of course. To be effective, a poem must, as we have spoken about, not just mean, but be.

In other words, it must embody in language what it is trying to express, just as the essay as a whole must "embody" the essence of who you are.

A great essay will not just describe who you are to the powers that be, but rather, take shape before them.

Let's take James Wright's poem "A Blessing" as an example. He might well have said: *I saw these two horses along the road. They were beautiful. Seeing them made me so happy I nearly jumped out of my skin.*

But he didn't.

Instead, he described the experience in such a way as to *take us through* it, so that we experience, when we read the poem, something of what he experienced in stopping to see those horses along the road.

> "Just off the highway to Rochester, Minnesota," Wright begins. "Twilight bounds softly forth on the grass./And the eyes of those two Indian ponies/Darken with kindness."

> Using similes, he brings the horses to life: "They bow shyly as wet swans." And "... her long ear/That is delicate as the skin over a girl's wrist."

> To express how moved he was by the experience, Wright ends the poem: "Suddenly I realize/That if I stepped out of my body I would break/Into blossom."

He doesn't need to say he is happy. He shows it by the way in which the poem is written.

Do you think Wright planned this poem out before writing it?

Do you think he made an outline?

Do you think he knew how it would end before he started?

I doubt it. That's not how great writing happens.

Don't think too much when you're describing something. Rather, looking above the surface of the water and below at the same time, let the words and images that come have a voice.

Here are some metaphors and similes that bring the image to life:

Her voice was like money.

His ears were like the folds of a rose.

It was as if I could see his thoughts when I looked in his eyes: They were clear but indecipherable like the refracted shards of colored glass trapped inside a kaleidoscope.

If you've heard it before, by the way, it's probably a cliché.

Cliché refers to an expression that has been overused to the extent that it loses its original meaning or novelty. Here are some examples of clichés.

- *Hit me like a brick.*
- *Bent out of shape.*
- *All ears.*
- *Fit as a fiddle.*
- *Make ends meet.*
- *Missed the boat.*
- *Tail between his legs.*
- *Gut-wrenching pain.*
- *Happily every after.*
- *When you have lemons, make lemonade.*

Make up your own descriptions.

These come from your inner experience and will be an accurate reflection of you, even if you yourself don't know how or why.

Remember, it's vividness, suspense, imagery, detail—the aliveness of your writing—that will keep your reader reading (and that's the point!).

Make it yours.

Bring it to life.

Again, I would read it aloud from beginning to end and ask yourself:

- Does it flow?

- Was I ever bored or distracted while I was reading it?

- Would someone reading it be able to come up with five adjectives that describe me from having read this essay? Are these adjectives broadly based or all pretty much the same?

- Does it tell a story?

- Is it interesting?

- Is the opening catchy?

- Is the writing original and in my own voice?

Ask yourself these questions. Answer them honestly. If you need to, go back and rewrite, even free write all over again.

Finally, once you feel your essay is truly as good as it can be, don't forget to proofread!

10. Proofreading

This is a crucial step. A beautiful essay full of errors is not going to fly. In fact, the Ad Com will feel disrespected if there are errors. I mean, really, this is your college essay! You have as much time as you need to get it right, right?

Here are some tips for proofreading:

1. As I have already mentioned, it's extremely useful to get another pair of eyes to look at your essay. Because you wrote it and it's your baby, it's easy to overlook typos, misspellings, and grammatical errors. You know what you meant to say, so you will have a tendency to fill in the blanks. Even though I proofread for a living, you can bet that the book that you are reading right now has been proofread by someone else. Reading

it backwards sometimes helps with typos and misspellings (if you're going to proofread it yourself.)

2. Beware of spell-check and auto-correct. (Recently I texted a friend and pressed "send" before I saw that the text read "Happy New Urea!") Also spell-check will not correct homonyms—there/their/they're, you're/your, to/two/too.

3. As I have previously suggested: Get some distance on it. Put your essay down for a few days and then come back to it with fresh eyes. This can really help, but still…Get another pair of eyes to look at it.

4. Refer to Appendix D, in which I provide some useful Dos and Don'ts.

The Slight Edge

If I had any suggestion at all for Jeff Olson—who, needless to say, did not ask my opinion in writing his book—I would have told him to make the book shorter, as the heft of his volume belies the simplicity of his message—the message which he knows so well—and which it takes many people a lifetime to figure out—"so much depends on so little."

Olson got it right when he called his book *The Slight Edge* for just this reason.

The difference between a life worth living and a life barely lived, a happy existence and one in which existence is mere survival, a college essay that stands out from the crowd and one that has the admissions committee snoring—is a significant, yet intangible, element that is both monumental, and yet requires just a little bit more elbow grease than anticipated, applied in just the right way—i.e., a slight edge.

Olson himself boils the mission of his book down to the following: He explains that his book is about "how you get from where you are to where you want to be."

Achieving the slight edge is not just about working harder; it is about working smarter—with the right strategies and in the right spirit.

How this applies to writing college essays is the point of this chapter.

What I would like to do here, thanks Jeff Olson, is summarize what he says in his book in a pithy package of important quotations—what he might call "pearls of wisdom"—and then make the connection from the concepts and ideas presented here to the art of writing the college essay.

Olson draws his wisdom from the great masters—the spiritual teachers, the pioneers and leaders—because he knows how important it is to stay with, and learn from, the winners, to use the insight of others, who have been successful, as a guide. He also knows that the greatest form of praise is imitation, and that it is extremely useful to use successful examples as models for your own writing and life.

When I see someone who is happy, successful, prosperous, generous and forward-thinking, I look closely at how they see the world, what they choose to focus on, maybe even more importantly, what they choose to ignore—and on how they choose to live.

I have learned great lessons from these people in the course of my life, and I am grateful to them for writing down what they discovered, so that people like me can learn both from their wisdom and from their mistakes.

Having read the book you have in hand, I'm sure you yourself could find the parallels between these words of wisdom and the writing process as I have outlined it here. In a way, you might find the following pearls of wisdom to be statements of the obvious, and obvious they may be, but they are not always easy to achieve.

Success is not the key to happiness. Happiness is the key to success. Albert Schweitzer

Another way to put this might be "Follow your bliss." Should you write in a way that is expected of you, sound sophisticated to satisfy what you think the Ad Com wants to hear? Or should you follow your heart, write about what most moves and inspires you, in a voice all your own, that reflects who you are and what is important to you? You know the answer to these questions.

Give me six hours to chop down a tree and I will spend the first four hours sharpening the axe. Abraham Lincoln

What Abraham Lincoln says here refers to *The Process*, to which I devote the lion's share of this book. Sometimes, as we have seen, an essay comes out all in a piece. No revision is needed. As easy as one, two, three. But for those moments when no such luck is available, it is good to have steps to rely on, a way to go from A to B. You will always need a bit of magic, but it is easier to find, if you start writing and see what comes out. Then you can always go back, and revise, elaborate, prune. But first, you must have something to work with, and know a little bit about what you're looking for. Otherwise, where would you find your tree and how would you know when to wield the axe? Or, in the words of other great thinkers:

I am a great believer in luck. The harder I work, the more of it I seem to have. Coleman Cox

Rome ne s'est faite pas dans un jour. (Rome wasn't built in a day.) Ancient French proverb

There must be something to this way of thinking because many great thinkers have echoed in their own words the same basic idea:

There is a natural progression to everything in life: Plant, Cultivate, Harvest. Jeff Olson

I might say: Prepare the soil; Toss out the Seeds; Let them Grow—free write. And, roll out the dough before you cut the cookies.

Do the thing and you shall have the power. Ralph Waldo Emerson

The formula for success is quite simple: Double your rate of failure. Thomas J. Watson, Founder of IBM

I took the [road] less traveled by and that has made all the difference. Robert Frost, *The Road Not Taken*

The journey of a thousand miles starts with a single step. Old Chinese Proverb

Sow an act, reap a habit. Sow a habit, reap a character. Sow a character, reap a destiny. Charles Reade

The difficult is what takes a little time; the impossible is what takes a little longer. Fritjof Nansen, Nobel Peace Prize 1922

And to add an aphorism of my own: In writing college essays, *one must sometimes get lost in order to get found.*

What exactly would a slight edge look like in the college essay writing process?

It could be taking a break and letting what you've written marinate; it could be letting your hair down and writing like your life depended on it; it could be going back one more time to make sure that when you read your essay, there's not a single weak moment in which you are bored; it could be getting good feedback from a trusted reader; it could even be scrapping what you have because it just doesn't fly.

The slight edge in the writing of winning college essays is about paying attention to the little things, putting energy into the process with faith that the product will unfold, making the ordinary extraordinary by bringing it to life, and going the extra mile, which means holding yourself to the gold standard of all writing: When you read it aloud, there is never a place where you begin to snore!

Whatever path you take, it is my hope that reading this book will have helped you just where you needed it most.

What's a Parent to Do?

So, you are the parent of a student writing a college essay.

Indeed it's a difficult position to be in. Your child, no longer a child, is struggling to write the single most important essay of his or her life so far, having never really been taught to do so, in order to get into you-fill-in-the-blank college in pursuit of his or her dreams. False starts, crumpled drafts, grunts and sighs—that's what your house has turned into! Losing sleep, energy, hope—both you and your child—something must be done!

Recently, I got a call from a dad in L.A. On a crackling line from Topanga Canyon, he explained his predicament to me:

"My son wants to go to UCLA," he said. "He has a GPA of 4.2 and 2300 on his SATs . UCLA is his first choice."

"Great," I said. "That sounds good."

"He needs to write good essays!"

"Yes, he does." I agreed. "The essays are really important."

"We heard you've gotten a lot of kids into UCLA over the years,"

"That's true," I said. "I have."

"Do you think you could help our son get in?"

"I sure can try."

"What do you charge per essay?" he said.

"What do you mean?" I said, hoping against hope he wasn't asking me what I thought he was asking me.

"Would you do it for $5,000?"

"I don't write essays for anyone," I said. "But I can help your son find a way to write an essay for himself."

The man hung up the phone.

I wish I could say this was the first time this had happened. It wasn't the first and probably it won't be the last.

Sometimes it's even subtler what goes on between a parent and their young adult child in this very important, sometimes harrowing process of writing college essays.

Writing is not easy—for anyone! And especially under deadline when it's really important.

There are ways to minimize the anxiety and maximize the depth and breadth of expression. This is what I've been writing and talking about—and doing—for years.

But, of course, parents are anxious too.

The best essays are the ones that come from the heart, that tell a story that needs to be told, even if it's a little rough around the edges. The best essays are original, personal, revealing, and honest.

Having someone breathe down your neck is not the best recipe for writing the best essay of your life.

Lucy Crawford (thanks, Lucy) wrote a really great article for *The New York Times* on this subject entitled "Let Go of the College Essay, and Let Your Teenager Speak for Herself." In it, she answers the question, "What's a parent to do?" quite gracefully:

> Perhaps you can tell your high school senior the things you most admire in her, list qualities and experiences, in case anything kindles. Perhaps you can say, What would you write if you knew we would never read it? and stand by that offer. You can just provide privacy and a cup of tea.

I couldn't agree more. Support, love, believe, and let your teenager write his or her heart out.

Get good help if you need it—not someone who will write the essay for the student, but someone who will help the student find his or her own unique voice, sometimes for the first time in his or her life.

Remember, the essay is more than just a ticket into college. It's the beginning of a journey of self-discovery and self-empowerment that needs to be honored.

You can help your child recall an event, if he or she asks. You can proofread the essay, if you are invited to do so. You can even suggest topics, if you don't care whether your son or daughter takes your suggestions or even lets you finish a sentence!

During the course of the initial consultation, when I meet parents and students for the first time, I make sure I say something like this: I cannot guarantee your son or daughter will get into the school of his or her dreams. I can guarantee that she will write an essay better than she could ever have imagined and that this essay will have what it takes to get her in. Whether or not she gets in, that's up to the gods. And so it is.

As I mentioned in the introduction, the college essay is probably the single most important piece of the college admissions puzzle, especially for stellar students whose academic record looks very similar to that of other stellar students. It's the only piece of the puzzle over which the student has complete control.

Does an excellent essay guarantee acceptance?

You know the answer to that question.

So, perhaps make yourself a cup of tea, too, and practice what your son or daughter must do in the process of writing his or her essay—the same thing you have had to practice at every stage in your child's development, now more than ever—the art of letting go.

Afterword: The Art of Writing the College Essay

> There is no how to do it, no how to write, no how you live, no how you die. If there were, nothing would live in the deep and very delicate chain of life. It is the doing that makes for continuance. It is not the knowing of how the doing is done.
>
> —William Saroyan, "Starting with a Tree and Finally Getting to the Death of a Brother," On Writing.

There is no *one* way to write—a college essay—or anything for that matter. And there is no *one* way to teach someone how to write. What I have offered here are insights I have had along the way as a writer, an editor, and a lifelong teacher of writing. They are by no means gospel. As Richard Hugo says in the introduction to his book *The Triggering Town: Lectures and Essays on Poetry and Writing*:

> You'll never be a writer until you realize that everything I say today…is wrong. It may be right for me, but it is wrong for you. Every moment, I am, without wanting or trying to, telling you to write like me. But I hope you learn to write like you. In a sense, I hope I don't teach you how to write but how to teach yourself how to write. At all times keep your crap detector on. If I say something that helps, good. If what I say is of no help, let it go. Don't start arguments. They are futile and take us away from our purpose. As Yeats notes, your important arguments are with yourself. If you don't agree with me, don't listen. Think about something else.

There are blissful days when nothing more is needed than a little space and time in which to put pen to paper or fingers to keyboard. Everything flows. Your keyboard and you are one.

And then there are days when nothing works. You try everything in the book, including hitting yourself in the head with it. My suggestion: Give up. Go out and play. Take a shower. Listen to some music. Text a friend. Eat a sandwich.

For the days when you're sitting in front of a white page or a blank screen and don't know what to do, I hope this book will be helpful.

At the end of the day, you want to feel that what you have expressed in your college essay really represents you—not your accomplishments, but your essence—and that your essay is more than the sum of its parts.

You want your readers to be unable to put your essay down. And, ultimately, you want the Ad Com to find itself incapable of saying no.

You want your essay to create an *experience* for your reader, not just provide a description, so that upon finishing your essay, he or she may feel what James Wright felt in seeing those horses along the road:

Suddenly I realize
That if I stepped out of my body I would break
Into blossom.

Appendix A: Sample Prompts

What makes you you are the experiences you have had in your life that have formed you. That's why so many of the essay prompts prompt you to think about this—what books you have read, where you have come from, what you most like to do, how you spend your time, whom you have encountered, what you like to think about, what's important to you, who's important to you, what you do when you're faced with adversity.

Sometimes the prompt is deceiving because you think it's only asking for description, but pure description with no action—by action I mean a moment unfolding in time and space—is a still life, and, while it may be beautiful, it will be unconvincing.

I would advise that when you come upon a prompt for the first time, see if you can think of actual moments in your life that would relate to what's being asked. And, of course, follow the steps outlined in this book.

Below are some sample prompts—including the Common App questions—for you to look at. You can always go to individual college websites or to the Common App site itself, if the prompts are posted, to get the most current questions when they come out. Most of the schools that use the Common App also require supplementary essays. The Common App website also lists those.

And then there are the "Whys." I always advise students to save them for last and, in them, offer an element of surprise. Don't tell evaluators what they already know about their school. Find a way to show them how strong your interest is and why it's a match. (Sophia Held's essay on "Why NYU?")

Recently I read a wonderful description of what the Whys are asking for on *Oberlin Blogs:*

> *The wording sometimes changes from year to year, but right now the question asks you to* "Please write a brief statement that addresses the following: Given your interests, values, and goals, explain why Oberlin College will help you grow (as a student and a person) during your undergraduate years." *We refer to this essay in our office as the "Why Oberlin?" essay, because we basically just want to know why you want to attend Oberlin, and what you think you're going to get out of the experience.*
>
> *Everybody's different, and we like differences, so we don't have one perfect answer to this question that we want everyone to approximate. We're looking to find out a bit more about who you are, and why you want to come to Oberlin. This is helpful to us in several different ways as we do our holistic review of your application.*
>
> *1) It gives us a better sense of who you are as a person and what you will add to the community.*
>
> *2) It gives us the opportunity to discover your level of enthusiasm for Oberlin and how much you're really interested in attending.*
>
> *3) It's another chance for us to evaluate your writing skills, and make sure that you can express yourself coherently and grammatically.*

From your perspective, this is the one place in your application in which you have the opportunity to directly make the case to the admissions officers about why they should admit you to Oberlin. The rest of your application is more general—it demonstrates why you should be admitted to college. This essay is the place to demonstrate why you should be admitted to Oberlin. We are a unique place, and we like to see that you have a sense of that, and that it's really what you want, and that you will add something positive to the Oberlin community.

Below are some sample prompts:

Common App

1. Some students have a background, identity, interest, or talent that is so meaningful they believe their application would be incomplete without it. If this sounds like you, then please share your story.

2. The lessons we take from failure can be fundamental to later success. Recount an incident or time when you experienced failure. How did it affect you, and what did you learn from the experience?

3. Reflect on a time when you challenged a belief or idea. What prompted you to act? Would you make the same decision again?

4. Describe a problem you've solved or a problem you'd like to solve. It can be an intellectual challenge, a research query, an ethical dilemma-anything that is of personal importance, no matter the scale. Explain its significance to you and what steps you took or could be taken to identify a solution.

5. Discuss an accomplishment or event, formal or informal, that marked your transition from childhood to adulthood within your culture, community, or family.

Tufts

Think outside the box as you answer the following questions. Take a risk and go somewhere unexpected. Be serious if the moment calls for it but feel comfortable being playful if that suits you, too. The required length for question 3 is 200–250 words.

1. Which aspects of Tufts' curriculum or undergraduate experience prompt your application? In short: "Why Tufts?" (50–100 words)

2. There is a Quaker saying: "Let your life speak." Describe the environment in which you were raised—your family, home,

neighborhood or community—and how it influenced the person you are today. (200–250 words)

3. Now we'd like to know a little bit more about you. Please respond to <u>one</u> of the following six questions:

A) "If you do not tell the truth about yourself you cannot tell it about other people," Virginia Woolf. Respond to Woolf's quote in the medium of your choice: prose, video (one minute), blog, digital portfolio, slam poetry…For media other than writing, please share a link (video can be submitted via YouTube but we recommend using a privacy setting) that is easily accessible.

B) What makes you happy?

C) Sports, science and society are filled with rules, theories and laws like the Ninth Commandment, PV=nRT, Occam's Razor, and The Law of Diminishing Returns. Three strikes and you're out. "I" before "E" except after "C." Warm air rises. Pick one and explain its significance to you.

D) Celebrate your nerdy side.

E) The ancient Romans started it when they coined the phrase "Carpe diem." Jonathan Larson proclaimed "No day but today!" and most recently, Drake explained You Only Live Once (YOLO). Have you ever seized the day? Lived like there was no tomorrow? Or perhaps you plan to shout YOLO while jumping into something in the future. What does #YOLO mean to you?

F) Boston is famous for its teams, its fans and its rivalries. Whether you are goaltending or cheering from the stands, celebrate the role sports plays in your life.

The University of California

Your personal statement should be exactly that—personal. This is your opportunity to tell us about yourself—your hopes, ambitions, life experiences, inspirations. We encourage you to take your time on this assignment. Be open. Be reflective. Find your individual voice and express it honestly.

As you respond to the essay prompts, think about the admissions and scholarship officers who will read your statement and what you want them to understand about you. While your personal statement is only one of many factors we consider when making our admission decision, it helps provide context for the rest of your application.

Directions

You will have 8 questions to choose from. You must respond to only 4 of the 8 questions.

Each response is limited to a maximum of 350 words.

Which questions you choose to answer is entirely up to you: But you should select questions that are most relevant to your experience and that best reflect your individual circumstances.

Keep in mind

All questions are equal: All are given equal consideration in the application review process, which means there is no advantage or disadvantage to choosing certain questions over others.

There is no right or wrong way to answer these questions: It's about getting to know your personality, background, interests and achievements in your own unique voice.

Questions & Guidance

Remember, the personal questions are just that — personal. Which means you should use our guidance for each question just as a suggestion in case you need help. The important thing is expressing who are you, what matters to you and what you want to share with UC.

1. Describe an example of your leadership experience in which you have positively influenced others, helped resolve disputes, or contributed to group efforts over time.

Things to consider: A leadership role can mean more than just a title. It can mean being a mentor to others, acting as the person in charge of a specific task, or a taking lead role in organizing an event or project. Think about your accomplishments and what you learned from the experience. What were your responsibilities?

Did you lead a team? How did your experience change your perspective on leading others? Did you help to resolve an important dispute at your school, church in your community or an organization? And your leadership role doesn't necessarily have to be limited to school activities. For example, do you help out or take care of your family?

2. Every person has a creative side, and it can be expressed in many ways: problem solving, original and innovative thinking, and artistically, to name a few. Describe how you express your creative side.

Things to consider: What does creativity mean to you? Do you have a creative skill that is important to you? What have you been able to do with that skill? If you used creativity to solve a problem, what was your solution? What are the steps you took to solve the problem?

How does your creativity influence your decisions inside or outside the classroom? Does your creativity relate to your major or a future career?

3. What would you say is your greatest talent or skill? How have you developed and demonstrated that talent over time?

Things to consider: If there's a talent or skill that you're proud of, this is the time to share it. You don't necessarily have to be recognized or have received awards for your talent (although if you did and you want to talk about, feel free to do so). Why is this talent or skill meaningful to you?

Does the talent come naturally or have you worked hard to develop this skill or talent? Does your talent or skill allow you opportunities in or outside the classroom? If so, what are they and how do they fit into your schedule?

4. Describe how you have taken advantage of a significant educational opportunity or worked to overcome an educational barrier you have faced.

Things to consider: An educational opportunity can be anything that has added value to your educational experience and better prepared you for college. For example, participation in an honors or academic enrichment program, or enrollment in an academy that's geared toward an occupation or a major, or taking advanced courses that interest you — just to name a few.

If you choose to write about educational barriers you've faced, how did you overcome or strived to overcome them? What personal characteristics or skills did you call on to overcome this challenge? How did overcoming this barrier help shape who are you today?

5. Describe the most significant challenge you have faced and the steps you have taken to overcome this challenge. How has this challenge affected your academic achievement?

Things to consider: A challenge could be personal, or something you have faced in your community or school. Why was the challenge significant to you? This is a good opportunity to talk about any obstacles you've faced and what you've learned from the experience. Did you have support from someone else or did you handle it alone?

If you're currently working your way through a challenge, what are you doing now, and does that affect different aspects of your life? For example, ask yourself, "How has my life changed at home, at my school, with my friends, or with my family?"

6. Describe your favorite academic subject and explain how it has influenced you.

Things to consider: Discuss how your interest in the subject developed and describe any experience you have had inside and outside the classroom — such as volunteer work, summer programs, participation in student organizations and/or activities — and what you have gained from your involvement.

Has your interest in the subject influenced you in choosing a major and/or career? Have you been able to pursue coursework at a higher level in this subject (honors, AP, IB, college or university work)?

7. What have you done to make your school or your community a better place?

Things to consider: Think of community as a term that can encompass a group, team or a place – like your high school, hometown, or home. You can define community as you see fit, just make sure you talk about your role in that community. Was there a problem that you wanted to fix in your community?

Why were you inspired to act? What did you learn from your effort? How did your actions benefit others, the wider community or both? Did you work alone or with others to initiate change in your community?

8. What is the one thing that you think sets you apart from other candidates applying to the University of California?

Things to consider: Don't be afraid to brag a little. Even if you don't think you're unique, you are — remember, there's only one of you in the world. From your point of view, what do you feel makes you belong on one of UC's campuses? When looking at your life, what does a stranger need to understand in order to know you?

What have you not shared with us that will highlight a skill, talent, challenge, or opportunity that you think will help us know you better? We're not necessarily looking for what makes you unique compared to others, but what makes you, YOU.

Stanford

The Stanford Writing Supplement Short Essays
Candidates respond to all three essay topics. (250 word limit for each essay.)

1. Stanford students possess an intellectual vitality. Reflect on an idea or experience that has been important to your intellectual development.

2. Virtually all of Stanford's undergraduates live on campus. Write a note to your future roommate that reveals something about you or that will help your roommate—and us—know you better.

3. What matters to you, and why?

Hampshire College

Supplemental Essay

All applicants must submit an analytical essay.

1. Analytical Essay/Academic Paper. We are interested in your ability to ask complex questions, think critically, synthesize information, and formulate your own conclusions through original analysis. Submit an academic paper you have written for a class in the past year.

We do not accept in-class essays, creative writing samples, journal entries, lab reports, and essays not written in the English language.

If you do not have an example which best represents your ability to write analytically, feel free to create and submit an essay on a complex question of your own design.

2. Proposed Program of Study (transfer applicants only). Please describe your academic interests and goals in one to three paragraphs.

You might include the types of courses you wish to take (although a listing of course titles alone is insufficient) and any independent projects, internships, or field studies you envision yourself doing. The Proposed Program of Study is not a contract; it is intended to help determine whether Hampshire is an appropriate place for you to continue your academic studies.

M.I.T.

One of the differences between the Common App and the MIT application is that we don't prompt for a single, longform essay. Instead, we ask our applicants to provide short (100-250 word) answers to five questions.

They are very simple, very straightforward, and this year, they go something like this:

We know you lead a busy life, full of activities, many of which are required of you. Tell us about something you do simply for the pleasure of it.

Although you may not yet know what you want to major in, which department or program at MIT appeals to you and why?

What attribute of your personality are you most proud of, and how has it impacted your life so far? This could be your creativity, effective leadership, sense of humor, integrity, or anything else you'd like to tell us about.

Describe the world you come from; for example, your family, clubs, school, community, city, or town. How has that world shaped your dreams and aspirations?

Tell us about the most significant challenge you've faced or something important that didn't go according to plan. How did you manage the situation?

Occidental College

Here's a peek at the Required Short Answer Questions for first-year applicants.

In the Short Answers section of the Occidental Member questions on the Common App respond to the following prompts:

1. There are thousands of colleges and universities. Why are you applying to Occidental? What influenced your decision to apply and what distinguishes it from your other choices? (175 words max)

2. While we realize your interests may change in college, what are your current academic and intellectual curiosities? (175 words max)

3. Our values are shaped over time. What learning experience transformed your thinking during your high school years? It could be a class assignment, a book, a film, an academic interaction—anything that inspired you to view an issue through a different lens and alter your opinion. (175 word max)

4. Everyone has a personality quirk. What's your idiosyncrasy, and how does it reflect your distinct character? (128 word max)

Princeton University

In addition to the essay you have written for the Universal College Application, please write an essay of about 500 words (no more than 650 words and no less than 250 words). Using one of the themes below as a starting point, write about a person, event or experience that helped you define one of your values or in some way changed how you approach the world. Please do not repeat, in full or in part, the essay you wrote for the Universal College Application.

1. Tell us about a person who has influenced you in a significant way.

2. "One of the great challenges of our time is that the disparities we face today have more complex causes and point less straightforwardly to solutions." Omar Wasow, assistant professor of politics, Princeton University; founder of Blackplanet.com. This quote is taken from Professor Wasow's January 2014 speech at the Martin Luther King Day celebration at Princeton University.

3. "Princeton in the Nation's Service" was the title of a speech given by Woodrow Wilson on the 150th anniversary of the University. It became the unofficial Princeton motto and was expanded for the University's 250th anniversary to "Princeton in the nation's service and in the service of all nations." Woodrow Wilson, Princeton Class of 1879, served on the faculty and was Princeton's president from 1902–1910.

4. "Culture is what presents us with the kinds of valuable things that can fill a life. And insofar as we can recognize the value in those things and make them part of our lives, our lives are meaningful." Gideon Rosen, Stuart Professor of Philosophy, chair of the Council of the Humanities and director of the Program in Humanistic Studies, Princeton University.

5. Using a favorite quotation from an essay or book you have read in the last three years as a starting point, tell us about an event or experience that helped you define one of your values or changed how you approach the world. Please write the quotation, title and author at the beginning of your essay.

Appendix B:
Adjectives That Describe
Personal Qualities

I am sure you can add to this list, but here are some good ones.

adaptable	brave	childlike
adventurous	bright	churlish
affable	brilliant	circumspect
affectionate	broad-minded	civil
agreeable	buff	clean
ambitious	callous	clever
amiable	calm	clumsy
amicable	candid	coherent
amusing	cantankerous	communicative
balanced	capable	compassionate
beautiful	careful	competent
bellicose	careless	composed
below average	caustic	conceited
beneficent	cautious	condescending
blue	charming	confident
blunt	cheerful	confused
bold	chic	conscientious
boisterous	childish	considerate

content	demonic	drunk
convivial	dependent	dull
cool	delightful	dutiful
coolheaded	demure	dynamic
cooperative	depressed	eager
cordial	determined	earnest
courageous	devoted	easygoing
courteous	dextrous	efficient
cowardly	diligent	egotistical
crabby	diplomatic	elfin
crafty	direct	emotional
cranky	dirty	energetic
crass	disagreeable	enterprising
creative	discerning	enthusiastic
critical	discreet	evasive
cruel	disruptive	even-tempered
curious	distant	exacting
cynical	distraught	excellent
dainty	distrustful	excitable
decisive	dowdy	experienced
deep	dramatic	exuberant
deferential	dreary	fabulous
deft	drowsy	fair-minded
delicate	drugged	faithful

fastidious	guarded	indefatigable
fearless	hardworking	independent
ferocious	helpful	indiscreet
fervent	honest	indolent
fiery	humorous	industrious
flabby	idiotic	inexperienced
flaky	idle	insensitive
flashy	illogical	inspiring
forceful	imaginative	intelligent
frank	immature	intellectual
friendly	immodest	interesting
funny	impartial	intolerant
fussy	impatient	intuitive
generous	imperturbable	inventive
gentle	impetuous	irascible
good	impractical	irritable
gloomy	impressionable	irritating
glutinous	impressive	jocular
good	impulsive	jovial
grave	inactive	joyous
great	incisive	judgmental
gregarious	incompetent	keen
groggy	inconsiderate	kind
grouchy	inconsistent	lame

lazy	miserable	outgoing
lean	modest	outspoken
leery	moronic	passive
lethargic	morose	passionate
levelheaded	motivated	paternal
listless	musical	paternalistic
lithe	naive	patient
lively	nasty	peaceful
local	natural	peevish
logical	naughty	pensive perceptive
long-winded	neat	persevering
lovable	negative	persistent
lovelorn	nervous	persnickety
lovely	noisy	petulant
loving	normal	philosophical
loyal	nosy	picky
maternal	numb	pioneering
mature	obliging	placid
mean	obnoxious	plain
meddlesome	old-fashioned	plain-speaking
mercurial	one-sided	playful
methodical	optimistic	pleasant
meticulous	orderly	plucky
mild	ostentatious	polite

popular	resentful	short-tempered
positive	reserved	shrewd
powerful	resigned	shy
practical	resourceful	silly
prejudiced	respected	sincere
pretty	respectful	sleepy
proactive	responsible	slight
proficient	restless	sloppy
proud	revered	slothful
provocative	ridiculous	slovenly
prudent	romantic	slow
punctual	sad	smart
quarrelsome	sassy	snazzy
querulous	saucy	sneering
quick	sedate	snobby
quick-tempered	self-assured	sober
quick-witted	self-confident	sociable
quiet	self-disciplined	somber
rational	selfish	sophisticated
realistic	sensible sensitive	soulful
reassuring	sentimental	soulless
reclusive	serene	sour
reliable	serious	spirited
reluctant	sharp	spiteful

stable

staid

steady

stern

stoic

straightforward

striking

strong

stupid

sturdy

subtle

sullen

sulky

supercilious

superficial

surly

suspicious

sweet

sympathetic

tall

tantalizing

tender

tense

thoughtful

thrilling

tidy

timid

tireless

tolerant

tough

tricky

trusting

unassuming

understanding

versatile

warmhearted

willing

witty

Appendix C:
Quick Guide to Writing
a Winning College Essay

Once you understand what a narrative essay is—that you shouldn't just list your accomplishments and that you cannot (usually) start writing your introduction first even though it appears first in your essay—I suggest you do the following

1. Bathe yourself in possibilities:
   A) Gather prompts

   B) Read amazing college essays of all varieties

   C) Read great writing

2. Happen upon significant moments. To do this, I suggest that you:
   A) List significant moments. Think of experiences that have changed you.

   B) Play the Five-Adjective Game.

   C) If neither A nor B works, interview yourself or have someone interview you. Or you can try, "Wishes, Lies and Dreams."

   D) If A, B, and C don't work, go back to bathing yourself in possibilities, thickening the plot, fertilizing the soil.

3. Free Write. Once you have moments, you are ready for the most important step in the whole process—The Free Write. There are no rules for The Free Write. It is free. Write whatever you can think of in relation to that "moment," in whatever order comes out. The only guidelines I would give you are to write in full sentences and to write much more than you could ever use.

If you start writing about a different moment than the one you began with, go with it. You may even want to take notes in the margin or open a new document to start a new idea.

4. Marinate. After you've written The Free Write, it's a good idea to take a brief break. Let it marinate for a few days. This is also a good time to show your Free Write to someone who can help you see what you're writing about and mark it with questions they have. Remember, you went through the experience and may tend to make assumptions about what people know and don't know.

5. Expand your Free Write. Try to develop and elaborate upon what you've written in The Free Write. Go back to your Free Write, figure out where the "blanks" are, and fill them in. Remember to roll out the dough, before you cut the cookies.

This is a good time to call in the W's.

- Where were you?

- When was this?

- Who were you with?

- What were you doing?

- How did you feel?

- What was important to you about that moment?

- Why do you think you remember it?

6. Marinate again. I would take a little break before going on to the next step.

7. Excavate. Go back to the Expanded Free Write. Make sure you've exhausted all possibilities and written as much as you can. If you have, start searching for a great opening sentence. Usually, if the sentence is really catchy and strong, it's a sign that it's significant as well. I call this "the tyranny of what works."

8. Create a rough outline. Having looked over your Expanded Free Write and picked an opening sentence, it's time to figure out where you would go from there, kind of like this: *I could start with that sentence, then speak about that moment, then say I hadn't wanted to go on the trip in the first place, then say why, then say that happened last summer too,*...and voila. Put numbers in front of each of these points, and you'll have a rough outline.

9. Lift and Drop. Go back again to your Expanded Free Write. Lift pieces of your Expanded Free Write and drop them into the slots laid out in your rough outline. Where you think you may need a transition, put [*transition*] in brackets so you can come back to it or write one on the spot if you can. Where you think you may need another *something* that you can't put your finger on, in brackets write [*Add something emotional/suspenseful/contextual/foreshadowing here*].

10. Revise. See with new eyes. Sweep through your essay from beginning to end. Fill in wherever there are missing details. Enliven the writing with interesting and active verbs. Make the language strong and vivid and alive. Have you said what you want? Does it make sense? Does it flow? Sweep from beginning to end, again and again, until you are satisfied you've made it as strong as you can. If yes, you have completed a rough draft.

11. Get feedback. Once you have a rough draft, you should put it away for a few days, while you read some other great essays and/or show it to your trusted reader. Probably at this point, you'll need once again to revise.

12. Proofread. Best if you get another pair of eyes to do this for you.

How to Structure Your Essay

There are infinite possibilities. What follows is just a suggestion:

Opening—drops you into a moment. *En medias res. The cold open.*

Backstory—explains the context around the moment

Reflection—expresses your thoughts/feelings/ideas about the moment you have just described, the story you have just told.

Development—develops the tension or conflict with another example

Reflection—once again, reflect on that example.

Conclusion—end with something that ties back in some way to the original moment and has a twist or lesson.

Appendix D:
Dos and Don'ts in the
World of Grammar

Do: Be yourself!
Don't: Use inflated, false, haughty language with big words to make yourself look good.

Do: Write the way you speak
Don't: Use a thesaurus. Instead, use words you're comfortable with.

Do: Use active verbs—Instead of *he ran quickly*, say *he dashed*.
Don't: Use adverbs and adjectives (much). *Quickly*, he opened the door. I *carefully* placed my test on the desk. I give my students three adverbs a year. Spend them wisely. Instead use active verbs!

Do: Use specifics. If you mention your dog, say its name. If you mention a friend, say her name. *Mrs. Plum in the Conservatory with a Wrench.*
Don't: Use gross generalities. *As everyone knows...People always think...*

Do: Write from your own experience.
Don't: Write about specific religious or political issues. People have varying opinions on the topics of sex, religion, and politics. I would generally avoid these three topics in a college essay. Again, there are exceptions.

Do: Vary sentence openings.
Don't: Start every sentence the same way or with "I." Start some with prepositional phrases: *In the morning, after I feed my dog...*Or participial phrases, *Having played an instrument for ten years, I...*" And be careful about starting sentences with the word "as." *As I was walking to school...As I turned to say goodbye.* You get two of those a year. Either take the as's out and say: *I turned to say goodbye,* or be more specific: *After packing up the bag I had just unpacked, I turned to say goodbye.*

Do: Vary sentence length. Mix it up—longer sentences with shorter ones. That'll keep your reader awake!
Don't: Put many long sentences back to back.

Do: Use dialogue rather than indirect discourse as much as you can.
Don't: Say what someone said without quoting them.

Do: Use fresh, original language.
Don't: Use clichés. If it's a saying you've heard before, opt for something more original.

Do: Bring it to life and make it clear.
Don't: Use generalities such as *obviously, clearly, somewhat, virtually, unquestionably, kind of, rather, quite, sort of…*

Do: Trim the fat
Don't: Use ten words where five would do.
Instead of: *Richard is someone who likes to tell everyone what he thinks about everything.*
Say: *Richard likes to say what he thinks.*

Do: Make specific distinctions.
Don't: Overuse *similarly* and *differently. My old school was different from my new one.* Instead, be specific: *My old school was bigger, but less rigid.*

Do: Use active voice. *Barry Bonds hit the winning run.*
Don't: Use passive voice: *The winning run was hit by Barry Bonds.*

Do: Be conscious of gendered nouns.
Don't : Use mankind, mailman, fireman. Instead use: humankind, mail carrier, and firefighter.

No-No's That Are Actually OK

Your fifth-grade teacher may have warned you against the following, but, actually, in a personal statement, which is what a college essay is, it's just fine.

You MAY start a sentence with *and* or *but*.

You MAY start a sentence with *because*.

You MAY (occasionally and deliberately) use a sentence fragment for effect. *He was my best friend. My go-to guy.*

You MAY use casual language. Instead of *I had not been prepared for this occurrence.* Just say, *I didn't expect it.*

You MAY use contractions (as seen above)

You MAY write a one-sentence paragraph. It can be very effective.

Appendix E:
Model Essays

Cat in the Hat Hat

First thing my last roommate, Emma, saw, was a girl with a *Cat in the Hat* hat sitting in the middle of the room. She wasn't expecting me. The room was chaos. She was embarrassed because of the mess, and guiltily hastened to fix it. At Emma's command, a swarm of people rushed into the room. One with a vacuum cleaner, another to pull out the smuggled air mattress, yet another to push the beds back to their original spots. Little did they know, the room was about to be a whole lot messier. Little did I know, these people would be my closest friends. I hope that I offered more than a warm body and an industrial fan that the room much needed.

Running around the hallways with a theatrical prop, I immediately ended up staging a fake battle with a wielder of an inflatable hammer as if I had been there all along. I ran through the hallways meeting everyone who crossed my path, starved for human interaction. We did normal things too: programming calculators, staying up late doing homework, playing cards, swimming, hanging out in downtown Palo Alto. I brought energy and entropy to a level of harmony. Some would say I'm reserved or introspective. I am. But that's only one side of the coin. My ideas are messier than the room I shared, crazier than the fake battles I staged. I'm alive. I want to enjoy my youth while I still have it.

Lizzy Wu

Las Tres Sofias

My grandmother bursts out laughing amidst a cloud of flour. She has accidentally dropped the bag on the floor in the frenzy of preparing dinner. As her giggles fill the air, I think about how often I see her smile. My mother watches my 'Abé' with admiration. The resemblance between mother and daughter is uncanny. They are both defiant and energetic and covered in flour! When I see them together, I see my future, and I know that the qualities I admire most in them, run through my blood. Together, we are 'Las Tres Sofias'—three generations of 'Sofias,' each adding ingredients to our collective legacy.

In this memory, my mother and my grandmother chat about our upcoming move to Hong Kong, where we now live, as they pass each other spices and spoons. *'Estarás bien Sofia!'* my grandmother exclaims. They are making *Bacalao, Croquetas de Jamon* and *Flan*—dishes that integrate my Mexican, Spanish and Cuban heritage. My mother occasionally scribbles in a black notebook, whose pages are stained with sauces and oils, and filled with recipes that define our family's history.

It seemed like there was never a moment in which my Abé wasn't smiling, especially when most of us would sigh and frown and feel like giving up. She had this unbelievable happiness to her that you would never expect from someone whose life had begun as hers had. Never one to hide her opinions, she was exiled from her home in Cuba at twenty-two for her involvement in anti-communist revolts. She left Cuba as a woman with a medical education and family, and arrived in her new home of Mexico with a wristwatch, the clothes on her back, and a degree that was no longer recognized. Spilled flour would not ruin her evening, as Fidel Castro would not ruin her life.

I see both of my cherished namesakes running around chopping and stirring, making a flawless Tuesday night dinner, because they are physically incapable of undertaking any task half-heartedly. This strong will transcends the kitchen: both my Abé, an oral surgeon, and my mother, an architect, break the paradigms of what is expected of women in our culture.

My mother has shown me that with blessings come responsibilities. She is single-minded, and what she fights for almost always benefits others more than herself. She never takes shortcuts because she only feels satisfied when she gives her all. This has not only been true in relation to little things, but in how she keeps our family together, in how she ran her business, and in how she has raised me.

The stride in her step, the joy in her laugh and the fire in her eyes are all qualities that she shares with her mother. Yet, after my grandmother's passing, my mother has had to face alone the task of teaching me how to be one of them, a Sofia. Through example, she has shown me how to be resilient, and take the combined strength of *Las Tres Sofias* and put it toward something bigger than myself.

The more I've grown, the more I have come to see the similarities between myself, my mother, and my grandmother. Like the two Sofia's who have given me my name, I seem also to possess an unflagging, sometimes unexplainable, dedication to whatever I undertake. As I navigate the uncertain road ahead, and strive to make a difference, I hope to make proud the women who have preceded me.

Much like the recipes in the sauce-stained notebook, the Sofias represent the places that the women in my family have been and are going. My name stands for a refusal to accept defeat and mediocrity. And as long as it is mine, I have a responsibility to carry on the faith, strength and passion that I have been given.

Sofia Mascia

Egyptian Rat Slap & Blueteeth

Here at our table is my aunt Jodi—a frizzy-haired, ninety-pound baker—and my Uncle Jim—a goofy, balding cartoonist who never fails to lighten the mood with a dirty joke. Across from them, my dad's twin, Aunt Robin, a scattered and energetic cardio electrophysiologist, is sitting next to my quiet and serious Uncle Doug, a clinical psychologist who always seems to know what everyone is thinking. Here they all are, gathered to celebrate my first day of high school, or "the best years of my life," as they like to put it. My dad's family sits on the right side of the table—every single one of them looking at papers that lay scattered among the breakfast dishes. If you saw them from a distance, it would seem that they were having a very animated conversation with one another, but as you get closer you can see the blinking lights of the Bluetooths behind their ears. When I turn my attention to my mom's side of the family, I see a playing card go flying across the table. A game of Egyptian Rat Slap has broken out and the whole table shakes with the excitement of the match. Even though both sides of my family are sitting two feet from each other, they might as well be two miles apart. For the first time in my life, I could see a glaringly clear image of the people who have shaped me, both the good and the bad, and that moment changed who I am. I began to contemplate who I wanted to be on this vast spectrum of lives and goals.

What I realized is that I want to have the same academic success that the right side of the table has, while being as down-to-earth and content as the left. At Macalester, I will bring to the table both sides of the table— my open mind, curiosity and love for new experiences and adventures, and my dedication, commitment to excellence, and unending desire for academic challenge and success. Unwittingly, my family brought into focus what is truly important to me—my desire to help the world , and the importance of having friends and family that will always be there for me while I'm doing so. These values inspire me to work passionately to gain both the knowledge and agency needed to right injustices, while creating and strengthening my community and relationships.   I won't lose sight of the unintentional lesson that my family shared with me that morning over blinking Blueteeth and impromptu card games.

Olivia Sterling-Maisel

Dendrochronology

My life has grown outward, rings on rings on rings. If you were to take a cross section, you would see many regular, consistent rings, representing wholesome years and inspired growth. But like a tree, whose maturation can be affected by fire, drought, fluctuating temperatures, or other stressors, so my life too consists of rings that are irregular, darkened not by early frost or insect infestations, but rather, by pressures in my family and my own internal struggles.

My earliest memory is of a fork coming at my face, as if my face were a dartboard. Sanath, my brother, is standing on a chair, laughing and pulling out more dinnerware from the cabinets. I was a year old and he was three. Knocked from my high chair to the ground, I remember being face-to-face with carpet, the color of oatmeal. When my brother was three, it was discovered that he had a rare form of epilepsy, from which he suffered seizures attacking his left frontal lobe.

In the first part of my adolescent years, I began realizing how others saw Sanath: a lanky kid, almost 5'8", wearing an oversized T-shirt with a Disney character on it, preferring to talk to children rather than adults. Lingering in the front of a cash register at Target, muttering to himself, and sometimes waving his hands in the air, having an intense debate with himself, maybe reenacting a scene from Tarzan, I see the looks directed at him. Parents usher their children past him quickly, and glance at him over their shoulders, as if worried he will create a scene of epic proportions.

"Mom, make him stop! He's talking to himself again!"

"Why can't you just understand? my mother sighs.

Photographs from when I was four or five show my brother and I swimming in pools of bright blue with webbed light reflections, clambering over train replicas at community parks in an area filled with wood chips, sharing space on the blue couch speckled with pastel yellow polka-dots, watching reruns of *Dragon Tales*, beaming up at the glowing screen. Polaroids of myself at three years old, nursing a sore elbow, tears running down my face. A tragic scene, until you note the skinny arm around my shoulder, providing a pillar for my childish sorrows. Time and time again, my brother is my champion, the biggest source of comfort in my life.

Recently, I read an article that describes how trees speak to each other. They interact to help each other grow, by warning each other of insect attacks or other environmental threats. I cannot help but wonder how my life interacts with Sanath's, and how his rings look, and even if I have helped in forming them. I wonder if, like the trees, my life force somehow speaks to my brother's, soothes him when he's upset, angers him at times, helps him survive. I wonder if you could read this in the rings of his life as clearly as you could read it in mine.

Surya Nair

Finding My Sea Legs

I still had one-third of the race left to go. Out of sheer fatigue, I began to slow down. My arms felt heavy in the water; my shoulders ached from overuse. I lost feeling in my hands and toes. Worse still, doubts raced through my mind. Who was I, a teenager, to believe I could swim ten kilometers in the cold and rough waters of the San Francisco Bay? Earlier that month, I had come home from practice just in time to pick up the phone. It was Mark Rosen, the director of the Bridge-to-Bridge race. "Because you're fifteen years old," he said in a hesitant voice, "before we create new legal documents for you, I want to be sure you've had enough training and experience." I heard the same doubt in his voice that I had heard in the voices of my parents..

I knew this would be the longest race I had ever swum. I also thought I was ready. As I dove into the fifty-eight-degree water just outside the Golden Gate Bridge, I felt tingling sensations. A quiet numbness crept through the rest of my body. At that moment, looking up at the bridge above my head, my goals and my feet kicked into high gear. I quickly got my arms into a rhythm, to move forward and keep my body warm. And then I was in the zone. When this happens, my mind wanders as my body does what it has been trained for years to do.

I have been swimming competitively year-round since age eight. Long ago I became accustomed to intensive practices, daylong swim meets twice a month, and a constant smell of chlorine radiating from my body. The water is a private space that has kept me balanced when my life tips to either side of the scale. It is a place of mind and body where I feel confident and capable with a strong sense of purpose. And so when I heard about the bridge-to-bridge swim, I couldn't resist. Whenever I thought about the possibility of swimming this race, a fire lit up in my heart that I could not ignore.

The Golden Gate behind me, I caught sight of the Palace of Fine Arts on my right and Alcatraz on my left. Although I only touched one jellyfish, I was thankful of what I could not see below. My dream was becoming a reality. The sun, casting beams through the bridge's cables behind the towers, was beckoning me. Yet the finish line was still a long way away.

Those last three kilometers pushed me more than I had ever thought possible. I was on my own. I had to remind myself why I was here at this moment and why finishing was important. I had made the decision to race and had spent years preparing for this moment. In spite of the fears of my parents, the worries of the race director, and even my own doubts, I needed to test what I was made of and see what I could do. Finally, as if I had suddenly found a hidden source of energy within, I powered through the last fifty strokes knowing how close I was to reaching my goal that was a ladder attached to a boat—the finish line.

The first female to finish, I was also the first finisher without a wetsuit, the third overall finisher, and the youngest participant in the race.

My heart was my guide throughout the swim. I grew up playing in San Francisco's Bay. It was here that I would come into my own. I could not let myself fail in the place where I learned to dream and soar. I needed to finish fast and finish strong in the waters from which I came.

Lucy Faust

Grandpa Stephen

Could the person who's influenced you most be someone you've never met?

Because my grandfather died before I was born, over the years I created my own legendary character from the pieces of information I was given. My mom often described her father's many positive attributes to me: She told me he was a great teacher, he was patient and generous, and that he loved math just as I did. What my mother told me about my grandfather became the seeds of my image of him, a figure larger than life. My Grandpa Stephen was more than just good at mathematics: In my mind he had a mathematical worldview. He was someone who saw the numbers behind everything, and because he understood the numbers, he understood it all. My mom told me about their many adventures traveling and visiting foreign places. In my mind, Stephen was an explorer. He wasn't content to stick to what he knew; he wanted to find and experience the novel and extraordinary. My mom often said she admired his humility. My Stephen was humble, and through this humility he was profoundly charismatic, and able to win over all those around him. He could find success because he could relate to people. He could quietly establish that he was the most interesting person at the dinner party. And I felt like I wanted to be like him.

It was not always this way. As a younger child, I didn't want to know anything about my grandfather. My mom told stories which held great personal meaning to her, but at first seemed random and scattered. I was often frustrated because I felt that she was trying to manipulate me with her narratives. "It really is too bad you never got a chance to know him," she often said to me. I thought she was trying to convince me to be just like him and to follow in his footsteps. When she told me that he was brought back to life in me, I didn't know what she meant and I didn't want to hear it. At that time, the most important thing to me was to find direction on my own.

But as I got older, I found myself wanting to know more about him. I wanted to better understand how my own story could resonate with this person whose name was passed on to me. One evening, I asked my mom if we could watch old footage of my grandfather's memorial service. As the tape rolled on, I found myself entranced. Occasionally, I looked over and saw my mom's eyes tearing up.

I clearly remember watching the procession of his fellow professors and colleagues and former students come up to the podium and confirm what I had been imagining: His methodical and reasoned approach to every problem and his mischievous obsession with solving them, his generosity of time and thought to all those who asked for it, his warm and ironic sense of humor. And I remember feeling certain that Grandpa Stephen could help me find the best in myself, to discover what I do well and how best to do it.

So I continue to look towards my grandpa for inspiration and as a guide to follow. And sometimes it feels like I'm looking right at him.

Skylar Powell

Heller Keller: A Place of Power

She was regarded as a saint, a miracle child who defied the bleak future that had once lay ahead of her.

But somewhere along her journey in the public eye, Helen Keller witnessed inequality, so she (very publicly) became a feminist, a socialist, a pacifist, and a supporter of the NAACP. The FBI began to keep a file on her. She had become an independent thinker, and she dared to speak her mind. She had become dangerous. Initially, when the world seemed to turn around and berate her, Keller stood her ground. However, when the American Foundation for the Blind told her that she had to either stop speaking so politically or end her work with the organization, she changed her mind. Keller's work with the organization had become important to her, so she made the decision to cease airing her famously radical beliefs in order to benefit her cause.

I admire Keller for daring to share her radical (and unpopular) worldview with a society that already didn't welcome the opinions of women, and I became upset when I learned of Keller's efforts to suppress her opinions. If I could speak to Keller, I would ask her if going "back in the closet" (vocally) later in her career brought back memories of being unable to communicate as a child. I would hope that she would reassure me that she made the decision from a place of power.

Bianca Rico

Mighty Minnows

"Come on! Really? Yoga music?" a fellow coach teases. I can barely hear over the clamor. Even in my third summer coaching kindergarten swimmers, I am still taken aback by their boundless energy. Yoga music sounds like a perfect antidote. "Put your hands on the floor," I say. "We're doing Downward Dog!" Determined to bring order to the situation, I assume the role of yoga instructor, putting both hands and feet on the floor in an upside down "V." The kids start laughing. Then, silence. As I look backward through my legs, I see thirty little bodies following my lead. Like clockwork, each child, hair still dripping from swim practice, is struggling to keep his or her balance. Only music and infectious giggles surround me. As we move through our flow, the swimmers are intrigued by every pose. Adults look on, shocked and delighted by the sudden hush.

Just eight years ago I, too, was a little swimmer running from the pool, ecstatic to be with the coaches for after-practice fun. Swim team was my home during summers growing up, and my love for swimming turned into a year-round passion. Now as summer team coach, I am immersed in the distinct smell of sunscreen and new latex caps reminiscent of my early years at the pool. My role has changed. I'm an orchestrator of the team itself.

A window opens on the interval between the child I was and my young adult self. As I catch a glimpse of that younger me, I can see the metamorphosis. Just like my swimmers, I was once too consumed with negotiating each moment to see the big picture. So how did I evolve from being one of these young swimmers to the role model I am now?

My first year on the team, at age six, I was in a group called "Mighty Minnows," named for the bursting energy inside our animated bodies. I paddled wildly down the pool, kicking with all my might, but barely moving forward. As an air breathing human in a liquid environment, I had to become an amphibian. With countless practices and words of encouragement, I gained control and autonomy. As my limbs grew, so did my attention to detail: where to put—and not put—my arms in the water, how to use my hands as paddles, my feet as fins. Steadily, my wild movements became self-directed. Practice, trial-and-error, until I found a way to glide effortlessly through the glassy blue. I was no longer splashing around in the shallow end, but navigating deeper waters, allowing my muscle memory to carry me forward—setting and achieving goals only previously imagined.

Now I am the motivating force peering over the pool deck at my own minnows who are taking my cues through their foggy, goggled eyes. Being a coach confers on me the responsibility of becoming a temporary buoy in the middle of the pool, a way station for tired legs. After sufficient rest and a quick pep talk, I am the wall they can push off of. On the deck, I become the jungle gym, as young swimmers beg for me to lift them skyward in backward somersaults. My supervisor, my fellow swimmers, and my own mighty minnows can count on me, and within the community that fostered my love for being a part of a swim family, I am now team Yogi, team player, and team leader. No longer a tadpole, I emerge from the pool fully formed.

Leila Schneider

Mudville

I used to be the mayor of Mudville—a small town nestled among the roots of a dying tree in the yard of my elementary school. My own little utopia began when two friends and I were playing outside after a particularly intense rain and were delighted to find the ease at which the drying mud in the schoolyard could be shaped into perfect spheres. By the end of that wet recess, our orbs of wet dirt had evolved into tiny beings—each no bigger than one inch in diameter—with names and personalities. Soon, more and more girls joined in on our mud game, and we began to create a tiny, fairy-like city in the ground for our mud creations. Mudville was a democracy—or so I wanted to believe. As founder, I called town meetings every day at lunch to vote on issues surrounding food supply, the latest materials that had come into bloom, and of course, our defenses against the enemy (boys). At the time, I saw my rise to power as a natural sequence of events. At the first town meeting, when we set up the rules of Mudville, I suggested that there be a leader to keep the town organized. As I described the mayor's various duties, I markedly pointed out the "coincidental" fact that I had already begun to "perfectly" carry out some of the future mayor's roles (if I had to say so myself!). Unfortunately, I realized (and must now confess) that under my reign, Mudville may have been more of a dictatorship than a democracy.

My first abuse of power occurred when I took control of the town's aesthetics. I rearranged my friends' mud ball houses when they were absent from school. Every time a friend took note of a slight difference in her house, I passed it off as an act of nature. "The wind was vicious last night," or "There must have been a rain." Once I tasted the glory of control, my appetite for power expanded, so I began to skew Mudville's "voting" processes by making up my own rules about each election.

"Anybody who doesn't share her dessert with the mayor today can't vote," I could be heard proclaiming. At the height of my tyrannical power-high—by this time, I was seven—I made the decision to control the population of Mudville by excluding one classmate, with whom I didn't get along, from participating in the town at all.

At the time, my second-grade self felt only a little uneasy about the way I was governing, but didn't quite recognize that I was exercising a dictatorship that cast a dismal shadow over the town.

The moment that I realized the true nature of my governing style didn't actually come until my sophomore year of high school, when I was walking out of a class in which I had learned about dictatorships. I bumped into one of my previous Mudville friends. With dictatorships—and now Mudville—on my mind, my uneasy memories of the town suddenly made sense.

At the end of my sophomore year of high school, I had several opportunities to take on leadership positions in the various clubs that I was a part of, and took those positions on with a new awareness. Now, I lead discussions with my school's Peer Help group and buildOn chapter by letting others talk, making sure that everyone's voice is heard, and making executive decisions only when necessary. My memories of playing with those little balls of mud at school have inspired me to want to influence people only in the most positive and equitable ways, but most importantly, they have ignited my passion for leadership and have helped me to realize that I am happiest when I am not basking in the glory of my power, but rather guiding others towards their own dreams.

Bianca Rico

There Are Cows in the Story

"I'm hungry," I said.

That's when the cows emerged. They came trampling out of the bushes, all six of them very annoyed and very pregnant. Will shrieked and scrambled up a tree.

"What's wrong?"

"I'm afraid of cows"

And that's when the calves came out of the bushes. The four of us had decided to go rafting in what became a very large flood, and wound up stranded on an island. I have always wanted to ride a cow, so I worked up my courage to approach one of the moms. Just as I tried to hop on her back, she decided to take a nap. After a few attempts to rouse her, I settled down too. I woke up to one of the babies licking my face. When we were finally able to swim back, we discovered a taco truck. After not eating for two days, the taco was incredible. Then I paused.

"Guys, look what we're eating!"

Following my gaze to the ground beef filling our tacos, Julian said,

"You mean who we're eating."

I thought about the cows on the island and we all put down our tacos.

"That's the only thing that has ever stopped me from finishing a taco," Connor said.

We cast the tacos aside and walked back home.

The moral of the story is that in the most unexpected circumstances, amid floods, rogue rafts, and pregnant cows, with a sense of play there's always a "taco truck" at the end of the tunnel.

Olivia Sterling-Maisel

Traveling is a Part of Me

Not till we are lost, in other words, not till we have lost the world, do we begin to find ourselves, and realize where we are and the infinite extent of our relations. —Henry David Thoreau, Walden

With my minimal Japanese skills, I attempted to bring smiles to the faces of people who had little to smile about. Minamisoma, a town of seventy thousand, was still recovering from the tsunami, earthquake and nuclear meltdown, which had befallen them almost three years before. Even though we had come to bring food, I had also brought a Polaroid camera with me. As I stood in front of a group of kids who waited for their photos to be taken, I heard them yell "見せて" (Misete! Show me!) and I gave them the5.4 cm-wide film printed with their smiling faces. After I left, they kept the food and photos, while I got to keep the memory of a time when I felt perfectly content.

When I look back on that experience, I am reminded of the place inside me that is awakened when I hit the road. When I travel, I am able to become who I really am—adventurous and creative. Luckily, because my parents love to travel—my mom spent the last year researching in Japan—I have had the opportunity to pack my bags and go abroad many times in my seventeen years. This past summer, I spent six weeks in Nicaragua running educational camps for local kids. Two summers ago, my first time traveling alone, I lived in the small community of Mogobane, Botswana with a host family. My time there was complicated, inspiring and distinct.

One particular day in Mogobane, I went with my fellow volunteers and a few kids from my community to explore a marshland nearby. From a distance we saw a white shape sticking out of the mud. As we got closer, we realized that a goat had gotten stuck. Struggling with our slippery, mud-caked hands, we tried to save it. At some point, I fell backwards into the vigorous suction of mud—known by locals as "quicksand"— only to have my shoe swallowed up by it. With much effort, we finally pulled the goat out to safety. The next morning, we hiked back at sunrise, but sadly found that our goat had not survived through the night.

As difficult and bizarre as this experience was, it still evoked in me the feeling I get when I'm traveling. It helps me see that life is not always about the outcome. Yes, the goat died in the end, which was tragic. But the experience made me feel more alive, which is what always happens when I leave the familiar world of my Bay Area home.

In my travels, I have noticed that too often we choose to notice the dissimilarities between ourselves and other people and places, instead of seeing how much we are all alike. For example, when I was in Nicaragua, I got to see a very different lifestyle, one where the women wake up before sunrise every day to make tortillas and four-year-old children walk home from school alone. However, the longer I stayed, the more I realized that these differences are trivial and the way we are connected is what really matters. This understanding makes me feel like I can be comfortable anywhere.

As a fourth-grader, I went camel trekking through the Arabian Desert in Jordan. Standing atop a red sand dune, ready to sprint down as fast as I could, I already knew, as I know now, that I was happiest halfway across the world from where I live. It is as if, living inside me, hidden and quiet when I am in my "real" home, is a spirit that yearns to be lost again in unknown places where new and different experiences await me.

Mera Freeman-Gerlach

One Road, Many Roads

Chicago author Nelson Algren said, "A writer does well if in his whole life he can tell the story of one street." Chicagoans, but not just Chicagoans, have always found something instructive, and pleasing, and profound in the stories of their block, of Main Street, of Highway 61, of a farm lane, of the Celestial Highway. Tell us the story of a street, path, road—real or imagined or metaphorical.

This is the place I can remember living since birth.

Sometimes I get flashes of a different abode, another time. A white-walled apartment with red oriental wall hangings and white cabinets. Tall chairs, a blue couch with a yellow pattern.

Yet, whatever that place was, it is long gone; here is what I have now. A tan duplex, with a tall lantern in the front yard, petunias, and more petunias.

The road in front of the house was long and winding, and cracked and faded to a light blue. As a first grader, the road went on forever and forever, for miles, perhaps even beyond. Who knew where the road ended? Recently, I drove by, and was surprised to see that the road extends for less than a mile. As a child, that same road extended for legions, and in dreams, covered oceans and continents…

In real life, on this road, there were people of all types living on my block. My neighbors were Egyptians. Across the street was a builder. Down the road was a boy with "disabilities," just like in my own family. Two houses down was the home of a twenty-something woman who introduced me to movies that she loved. She moved soon after I met her, but I still remember her clear blue eyes. She showed me a small part of the world though her television. A few months afterward, we found ourselves moving to a larger house about three minutes away.

The day of our move, our neighbors waved as we backed out of the driveway. Right, left, a few minutes straight, and we were at our new house. Even though our new house was only three blocks from our old home, it felt like worlds away, quieter and the houses were farther apart, feeling forbidding and aloof. Not long after moving into our new house, we found ourselves on a plane to India, visiting our grandparents. Humid, rainy, hot. India was a familiar place to me. From the moment I got off the airplane and landed in the airport, everything around me had a familiar smell. It reminded me of the smell that came from my father's suitcase after he returned from trips to India, visiting his own parents. Even after I reached the dusty, winding road to my grandfather's house, atop a hilly garden, I could smell spices that were common in my mother's kitchen in Chicago. Paprika, turmeric, chill powder. Smells like home. The dirt road leading to the house was a rusty red, and after a while, morphed into a proper brick road that winded into the open garage. Right next to the open garage was a beautiful garden, full of roses, vines, and old, old trees. There were so many memories surrounding the garden, and the two old mango trees.

When I was younger, about eight, there was a flamboyantly blue swing suspended from one of the sturdier branches, and we looked at it with stars in our eyes. There was no better transportation to reach our dreams. Another swing was in the back of the house, but its charm disappeared once we discovered snakes hidden in the bush behind it, ready to strike. The trees were a source of entertainment once the mangoes were ready to gather, and my brother and our younger cousins were permitted to scramble up ladders, grab however many we could fit in a basket, and proudly present them to our mothers. Beyond the small garden and its pristine white wall, there is also a stretch of land that belongs to my grandpa. There are rows of fruit trees and greenery, and you can spy the winding, rusty red road and the gate leading to the outside world of bustling auto rickshaws and street vendors.

It seems like many roads, but it was one road, really, from my first memory, the tan duplex, to this very house from which I write to you now. From a neighborhood of all sorts of people, to plucking mangoes form ladders, every step I took along the way gave me new perspectives on the world. The road ahead seems unclear from this point on. However it is mine to walk, and even if it is full of twists and turns, my stepping stones will be the roads my feet have already known.

Surya Nair

Appendix F:
Trouble-Shooting Guide

Below I have listed some of the most important highlighted sections of the book. If you have specific questions, you can go to the general area in the book where these questions will be answered.

What is this book about?—15

Who are you, Gabrielle Glancy?—13

What makes you think you have anything useful to tell me about writing my college essay?—13

For whom is this book written?—16

How is this book organized?—19

What's the difference between Product and Process?—19

What is the experience of people on the Ad Com who read college essays?—5

Do the college essays really matter?—7

Are they as important as the GPA and/or SAT/ACTs?—10

What makes a great essay great?—3, 11, 42

Does it help to look at model essays?—25

What should you write about? What topics can college essays be about? -47

What is a personal essay?—36

Why can't you just say who you are and what you've done directly?—37

What kind of information about you are colleges looking for?—28

How is the college essay different from a five-paragraph essay?—36

What is a narrative essay?—36

Why do colleges want narrative essays?—37

What is a story?—39

What does "Show, Don't Tell" mean?—25

How do you bring a story to life?—32

How do you choose a topic?—47

What are the very first steps I should take in writing my essay?—48

What is a Free Write?—80

How do I write a Free Write?—81

What is the Five-Adjective Game?—57

How do I choose a moment?—54

What do I do after I've completed a Free Write?—91

If I don't know what to write about, what do I do?—52

If I'm stuck, what do I do?—70

How do I prepare myself to start writing?—65

How do I expand on my Free Write?—91

Once I have an Expanded Free Write, how do I form it into an essay?—95

How do I revise my essay?—103

How do I proofread my essay?—120

How do I know if my essay is good enough?—120

What kind of language makes a strong essay strong?—44

If you're a parent reading this, what do you do to help your son or daughter through this process?—123

About Gabrielle Glancy

Former Admissions Director, Series Editor of *Best College Essays*, and published in *The New Yorker*, New Vision Learning's Gabrielle Glancy has been in the business of helping students realize their dreams for almost thirty years. With a knack for knowing just the right formula to help high school students succeed where they have struggled and get in where they want to go, she is one of the foremost professionals and innovators in her field. Headquartered in the Bay Area, Gabrielle Glancy is well known all around the world for her college admissions expertise.

Other Books
by Gabrielle Glancy

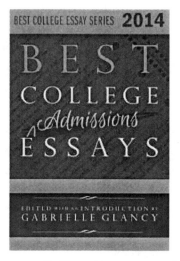

Best College Essays 2014
by Gabrielle Glancy

CPSIA information can be obtained
at www.ICGtesting.com
Printed in the USA
LVOW12s2116171016
509110LV00001B/164/P